HENRY WARD BEECHER
AS HIS FRIENDS SAW HIM

The Pilgrim Press

NEW YORK   BOSTON   CHICAGO

Presswork by H. M. Plimpton & Co., Norwood, Mass.

A FOREWORD

WE have gathered into these pages views of Henry Ward Beecher by men who lived in the atmosphere of Plymouth Church as he created it and as it has survived him, such men as Lyman Abbott and Rossiter W. Raymond; by men whose genius has received shape and direction at his hands, such as Gunsaulus and Hillis; by men who felt the impulse of his power over their childhood and youth, such as Edward Bok and R. D. Mallary; by men who have felt the breath of his inspiration in other lands and through his books, such as W. J. Dawson and A. B. Penniman; and by those who have known and loved him in their various spheres of service, such as Julia Ward Howe, Amory H. Bradford and John R. Howard.

The time in which this service could be done as it is done here is swiftly passing away. Year by year the circle is narrowed of those who knew Mr. Beecher intimately. Already a generation has reached middle life to whom he is known, if at all, only as a genius of a former period of our history now separated by much more than the mark which divides the nineteenth century from present affairs. The composite picture here given is in a sense new, for we believe it is the first collection which has been made of the carefully recorded impressions of so many of his personal friends, disciples and admirers. It is not likely that such a collection will again be attempted. With thousands who acknowledge a great debt to Mr. Beecher we are grateful to those who have made it possible for us thus to bring him again before us, in his preparation for his life-work, in his pulpit, on the platform, at his study desk, in the homes

50665

where he loved to visit, in his journeys to other lands, in
the circle of his intimate friends, and in his solicitous care
for young men.

The indescribable power of his oratory can be appre-
hended only by those who have heard it. In childhood and
manhood we, listening to him, have felt the electric thrill
passing through crowded audiences as they responded to
the spontaneous outflow of his great mind and heart keyed
to such exquisite harmony of human sympathy that voice
and words and action and thought made a grand diapason
which seemed to gather spirit, mind and body up into an
elysium of exultant faith and courage.   The power of
Mr. Beecher's personality cannot be reproduced.

But it is a satisfaction to find that after the personality
has become only a fading memory, Mr. Beecher abides with
us as a prophet of the first order, whose insight into truth
is more clearly recognized now than when he was living.
His wisdom has survived his personal magnetism, and the
generation which succeeds his accepts what he taught with
greater confidence than the generation which heard him.
He thought it advisable to withdraw as a minister from
official fellowship with his brethren in order that they
might not bear the responsibility for what he said.   But
the Beecher of twenty years ago would be received into full
fellowship to-day with little question and abundant honor.

The twenty-nine names inscribed in our National Hall
of Fame include three clergymen, all Congregationalists.
Their widely diverging teachings and types may, we trust,
prophesy as varied service of our historic denomination in
the future as it has rendered in the past.   Jonathan Edwards,
William Ellery Channing, and Henry Ward Beecher were as
far apart in theology as the East is from the West.   But
in their insight into the character of God and experience
of personal communion with him they stand close to one
another.   In sympathy with men and in interpreting to them

God, whom he beheld and knew, the greatest of these three was Beecher.

The pictures presented are not less notable than the contributors. Never has there been such a complete photographic reproduction of Mr. Beecher himself and of persons and places associated with him. The first portrait is said to be the last one of Mr. Beecher, taken by Elliot and Frye, in London, in 1886. The photographer stopped Mr. Beecher as he and Major Pond were going out of the gallery, saying: "Stop right where you are, Mr. Beecher. Don't move a muscle." It was issued for the first time in this country in the volume entitled, "Best Thoughts of Henry Ward Beecher," published by H. S. Goodspeed, of New York, to whom we are indebted for the opportunity of reproducing it. The photograph on page 10, by Rockwood, of New York, is also a late one, and appears as the frontispiece in Lyman Abbott's biography of Beecher, recently issued by Houghton, Mifflin and Company. Earlier pictures of Mr. Beecher have been gathered from many sources, and we are particularly indebted to Mrs. Frances L. Pratt, of Brooklyn, a long-time member of Plymouth Church, for suggestions and for the loan of rare photographs.

SALIENT DATES IN BEECHER'S LIFE

1813, June 24.   Henry Ward Beecher born in Litchfield, Connecticut.

1834.   Graduated from Amherst College.

1837.   Graduated from Lane Theological Seminary, Cincinnati, Ohio.

1838, November 9.   Ordained at Presbyterian church, Lawrenceburg, Indiana, having supplied the church from May, 1837.

1839, July 31.   Installed at Indianapolis, Indiana.

1847, September 19.   Dismissed from Indianapolis.

1847, October 10.   Installed at Plymouth Church, Brooklyn, New York.

1878–1887.   Chaplain of the Thirteenth New York Regiment.

1887, March 8.   Died at Brooklyn, New York.

TABLE OF CONTENTS

Church in Indianapolis in which Mr. Beecher preached

Church in Lawrenceburg, Ind., where Mr. Beecher first preached

ESTIMATES

OF BEECHER

From a photograph by Rockwood.   Believed to be his latest portrait

HENRY WARD BEECHER AS A CITIZEN

By Rev. Lyman Abbott, D.D.

Henry Ward Beecher was primarily a preacher of the gospel. He reiteratedly declared that his purpose in life was to bring men to a knowledge of God and a likeness with God, through Jesus Christ, the Saviour of men. He was a political reformer only because he believed that the gospel was social as well as individual; that the object of Christ was the reconstruction of society through the reconstruction of the individual; that to preach the gospel meant to proclaim the redemption of society, as well as the redemption of the individual, by an application to all social as to all individual problems of the principles and precepts inculcated by Jesus Christ.

Mr. Beecher is known as a brilliant orator, who employed the resources of wide reading, broad sympathy with men, vivid imagination and a devout emotional nature, coupled with extraordinary rhetorical and elocutionary gifts, in arousing the consciences and the affections of popular audiences, and directing them in channels for the promotion of nobler living. But the study of his political life shows also statesmanlike qualities: a clear understanding of current issues, a grasp of great political principles, and a prophet's perception of the direction in which lay the way to future peace and prosperity. These qualities are especially illustrated by his action in the

11

three great epochs of the national life in which he
took a notable part — the antislavery campaign, the
Civil War, the reconstruction period.   Within the
limits of this article I can but hint at certain mani-
festations of these qualities in these several epochs.

I.   THE ANTISLAVERY CAMPAIGN

Mr. Beecher is often called an Abolitionist.   If by
Abolitionist is meant one who desired the abolition of
slavery, the appellation is deserved ; if by Abolitionist
is meant one who agreed with William Lloyd Garrison
and Wendell Phillips, in the program which the former
kept at the head of The Liberator, he was not an Abolitionist.   He did not advocate "immediate unconditional
emancipation " ; he did not believe that " slaveholders,
slave-traders and slave-drivers are to be placed on the
same level of infamy and in the same fiendish category
as kidnappers and manstealers" ; he did not believe
that "the existing Constitution of the United States
is a covenant with death and an agreement with hell " ;
he did not believe in "no union with slaveholders."

His antislavery principles had their first clear
enunciation in an editorial published in The New
York Independent in the winter of 1850.   The occasion of this editorial was the compromise measure
introduced into Congress in January of that year for
the settlement of the slave question ; the principles
of the editorial were those incorporated in the platform of the Republican party, six years later, on
which, four years after that, Abraham Lincoln was
elected.   In this editorial Mr. Beecher declared, some
years before Abraham Lincoln and some weeks before

William H. Seward, the irreconcilable conflict between slavery and liberty, but he declared also his adherence to the Constitution, his loyalty to the Union, his belief that slavery was to be overturned, not by withdrawing from the Union, but by remaining in the Union and resisting the further extension of slavery.

The Garrisonian Abolitionists were the first secessionists; they sought to dissolve the Union in the interest of abolition. The Southern secessionists, ten years later, sought to dissolve the Union in the interest of slavery. Mr. Beecher believed that the forces in the Union for liberty would prove stronger than the forces for slavery, and to the awakening of those forces he addressed himself through the ten years of antislavery campaign — 1850–60.

It is true that he invited Wendell Phillips to lecture in Plymouth Church; it is true that he spoke on the same platform with William Lloyd Garrison. But he made it perfectly clear in speech, sermon and editorial that he believed that the North shared with the South in responsibility for slavery; that it could not escape that responsibility by withdrawing from the Union; that, despite some imperfections, the Constitution was a noble document, framed in the interest of freedom, not of slavery; and that, in the Union and under the Constitution, slavery could be so circumscribed that eventually it would die of inanition. When, therefore, John Brown attempted his disastrous raid into Virginia, Mr. Beecher was not among those who applauded him. "I protest," he said, "against any counsels that lead to insurrection, servile war and bloodshed. It is bad for the master and bad for the

slave, bad for all that are neighbors to them, bad for
the whole land — bad from beginning to end."

On the other hand, when the experiment of "squat-
ter sovereignty" was instigated by Mr. Douglas, and
the question whether Kansas should be a free or a
slave state was made dependent on the character of
its population, Mr. Beecher took an active part in
promoting emigration to Kansas of a quality of citizens who would carry with them a free school, free
labor, free press, and so a free constitution. He did
this at the time when the Abolitionists, with whom
public opinion has so often associated him, were de-
nouncing the Emigrant Aid Company as "a great
hindrance to the cause of freedom and a mighty
curse to the territory," and maintaining that "the
fate of Nebraska and Kansas was sealed the first
hour Stephen Arnold Douglas consented to play his
perfidious part."

History has so conclusively demonstrated that the
Abolitionists were wrong and the Kansas emigrants
were right, that the country has almost forgotten that
there was any issue between the two; history has so
conclusively proved that if the Abolition secessionists
could have had their way and induced the Northern
states to withdraw from the Union, they would simply
have played into the hands of those who were endeavoring to form a great slavocracy, extending west to the
Pacific Ocean and south into the Central American
States, that we have almost forgotten that such a
policy was ever seriously urged upon the people of
the North.

Mr. Beecher as a young man
From a painting now owned by Mrs. Tenny, of Lexington

II.   THE CIVIL WAR

In a similar fashion the nation has gladly forgotten
the spirit of compromise, not to say cowardice, which
threatened the North after the election of Mr. Lincoln;
we have forgotten that time of confusion, contradict-
ory counsels, conflicting currents, in which even so
eminent an antislavery man as Mr. Seward hoped to
find some way out by compromise, so influential a
journal as The New York Tribune said that "if the
Cotton States decide that they can do better out of
the Union than in it, we insist on letting them go in
peace," and so clear-headed and loyal a statesman as
Charles Francis Adams advocated the summoning of
a conference and the shaping of a compromise for the
purpose of preventing the Border States from casting
in their lot with the Confederacy.

In all this time of confusion and contradiction,
there were two men who never for a moment lost
sight of the one guiding principle, that concession
should nevermore be made to the slave power under
any pretext whatever, be the consequences what they
might.   These were the silent man at Springfield
and the eloquent man in Brooklyn, neither of whom
for an instant hesitated.   In his sermon preached
November 29, 1860, "Against a Compromise of
Principle," Mr. Beecher vigorously condemned all
such concessions.   Speaking, as to the South, from
his pulpit, he said : —

You shall have the Constitution intact, and its full
benefit.   The full might and power of public sentiment in
the North shall guarantee to you everything that history
and the Constitution give you.   But if you ask us to aug-

ment the area of slavery, to coöperate with you in curs-
ing new territory; if you ask us to make the air of the
North favorable for a slave to breathe, we will not do it.
We love liberty as much as you love slavery, and we shall
stand by our rights with all the vigor with which we mean
to stand by justice toward you.

These words sound like commonplaces now, but
they were uttered when Northern pulpits and Northern
presses were clamoring for some impossible compromise, when Congress was debating half-way measures,
when timid men were endeavoring to contrive some
platform of concession to slavery and secession that
would postpone the inevitable conflict, when the radical Abolitionists were advising to let the erring sisters
depart in peace. Of his eloquence in the later epoch,
stirring the heart and sustaining the courage of the
North, undaunted under disaster and defeat, I need
not speak here, for I am speaking of Mr. Beecher's
wisdom as a counselor, not of his eloquence as an
orator.

For the same reason I need not speak of those
marvelous addresses in England, which contributed
so largely to prevent English interference and did so
much both to arouse and to express the public sentiment of the common and unrepresented workingmen
of England, and so much to prepare the way for that
unofficial Anglo-American alliance which has grown
up within the last few years, to the satisfaction of
all right-thinking men on both sides of the water.

III. THE PERIOD OF RECONSTRUCTION

In the third epoch, that of reconstruction, Mr.
Beecher exhibited the same prophetic and statesmanlike quality. The problem of reconstruction, as it

presented itself to the people of the North at the close of the Civil War, was a very difficult and perplexing one. It is not strange that the best minds differed respecting the best method of its solution; even to-day men are not agreed what course should have been pursued. That great evils grew out of the course that was pursued does not prove that it might not have been the best. The nation was like a man in the middle of a swamp; turn which way he will he cannot get out without muddy and perhaps torn clothes, perhaps scratched and bleeding face and hands. But the fundamental principles which Mr. Beecher laid down seem clearer now in the light of history than they did when he first propounded them.

While still the question was open in the country whether the war for secession should be regarded as anything else than gigantic acts of mob violence, which left the states unimpaired to return under their old constitutions when the mob had been quelled, he took in his Fort Sumter address the ground that the United States are one and indivisible, that the states are not absolute sovereigns, that liberty is indispensable to republican government, and that slavery must be utterly and forever abolished.

These principles will seem to Northern readers alphabetic, but not so alphabetic as some other principles which he laid down almost simultaneously: that the North should do nothing to impair the self-respect of the South; that it should not demand conversion from secession as a matter of political opinion, but only consent that secession is forever disallowed as matter of practical result; that it should not wait for any

Birthplace of Mr. Beecher, Litchfield, Conn.

further guarantees for the future, the utter destruction
of slavery being all the guarantee necessary; that the
negro should have all civil rights, but as to suffrage,
that might be confined to a few, as, for example, to
"those colored men who bore arms in our late war
for the salvation of this Government"; that universal
suffrage might well wait upon the processes of educa-
tion; that the South should not be treated as a pagan
land to which missionaries must be sent, but as part of
a common country to which aid must be sent by the
richer and more prosperous section; that in all philan-
thropic and educational work in the South "our heart
should be set toward our country and all its people
without distinction of caste, class, or color."

The maintenance of these principles then subjected
Mr. Beecher to suspicion and rancor in the North, just
as he had been subjected to suspicion and rancor by
his vigorous antislavery sentiments ten years before.
Even to-day a radical remnant condemns the same
sentiments, now grown more widespread and popular.
To me it appears that his counsels were as wise as his
spirit was fraternal, and that in the period of reconstruction he showed the spirit of a statesman as truly
as in the period which preceded he showed the spirit
of a prophet and a reformer.

Mr. Beecher's greatness conceals his greatness.
His wit and humor, his imagination, his emotional
power, dazzle and sway men. While they are under
the charm of his personality they do not stop to con-
sider whither he is carrying them; when they look
back they do not know who has carried them, and so
unconscious has been the transference that often they

are unaware that it has even taken place. But I
believe that if the speeches of Mr. Beecher could be
denuded of the elements which made them powerful
as orations, if the great fundamental political principles which they embody could be epitomized in these
as unemotive and unimaginative as those of Martin
Luther, they would show that their author possessed
statesmanlike qualities which give him rank among the
eminent political counselors and leaders of the epoch
in which he lived.

(1) *At 23 years of age.* (2) *At 30.* (3) *At 40.* (4) *At 50.* (5) *At 65.*

THE RULING IDEAS OF HENRY WARD BEECHER'S SERMONS

By Rev. Newell Dwight Hillis, D. D.

Mr. Beecher published approximately seven hundred sermons, representing fourteen out of fifty preaching years. He published two volumes when he was fifty, gathering up forty-eight fugitive sermons that had been printed in pamphlets and newspapers; two volumes when he was fifty-two, sermons illustrating his various moods and methods. At fifty-five he began to publish one sermon each week, a publication that was continued until he was sixty-two; in his seventieth year he founded The New Plymouth Pulpit, and continued it for two years; at seventy-three his sermons preached during his summer's visit to England were printed; and he also left some twenty-five sermons published in The Christian Union but never put in book form.

His output, therefore, includes some twenty-four volumes of sermons — sermons biographical, doctrinal, philosophical, narrative, imaginative, and expositional; sermons written sometimes from the viewpoint of reason, sometimes from the viewpoint of persuasion and argument, sometimes from the viewpoint of inspiration and hope, but always with the purpose of convincing men of sin, persuading men from sin, the development of faith in God and love for Christ, and the building up of a Christlike character. From

23

twenty-five to forty years of age he wrote with great
care one sermon a week.   During this time, he tells
us, he was an apprentice, learning his trade.   Very
early he decided that the only way to learn how to
preach was by preaching.   Having, therefore, written
his Sunday morning sermon for his own people in
Indianapolis, on Monday he started out, and repeated
that sermon every night in as many different schoolhouses in the country round about.   In 1844 he
preached once every day for ten months in rural dis-
tricts and little villages, and a few sermons of that
epoch have on the first page the names of from ten
to thirty schoolhouses and churches where they were
preached.

At seventy-three I heard him say : "What if the
great orators and lawyers and statesmen were to try
to learn to speak by speaking on one day of the week?
What if a great singer should attempt to develop a
voice by singing one hour on Sunday and then never
opening the mouth until the next Sunday?   The only
way for young men to learn how to preach is to preach.
I question whether God himself could make a preacher
out of a man who opens his mouth one day and then
keeps his mouth closed during the next six days."
But Mr. Beecher was not simply a preacher who mas-
tered his art by practising it ; he was also a tireless and
accurate student, reading along the line of the theme
on which he was going to preach, and he continued to
do this until he was about fifty, at which time he had
accumulated between five and six thousand volumes.
Contrary to the usual opinion, also, few men in the
American pulpit have been better grounded in the-

" The man of many moods "

ology, philosophy and the apologetics of his era. To
the very end his library was singularly rich in theology,
philosophy and the relations between the new science
and religion.

Until he was thirty years of age he was under the
influence of his father, Lyman Beecher, and his interest in theological problems was kept at white heat
through the discussions of his brothers, who were
preachers. He tells us that for four years his father,
Professor Stowe, his brother Edward, and the other
three brothers, not to mention his sisters, who were
passionately fond of theology, gathered around the
dinner-table, and there continued, sometimes for two
and three hours, forgetting to eat, because they could
remember nothing but theology, the problems of Calvinism, and the discussions that were on between the
Old and New School Presbyterians. For thirty years
Mr. Beecher breathed no air but the air of theology.
Theology was the bread that he ate, theology was the
water that he drank, theology was the very blood in
his veins. He tells us that he knew the arguments
of the Puritan theologians, like John Owen, of all the
New England theologians, and of the Old School theology taught at Princeton and the New School of Calvinism taught in Lane — knew them so that he could
recite them forward and backward. He could play
with the arguments as a juggler keeps nine balls in
the air.

In 1875 a friend spoke to him about a certain
preacher who prided himself on his theological posi-
tions, and had said that Mr. Beecher knew nothing
about theology. Mr. Beecher replied, " When he has

preached theology for twenty years, as once I did, he
will through preaching master it, instead of being mas-
tered by his knowledge, as a big pile of green wood
masters the fire that smolders beneath." The fact is,
Mr. Beecher rejected the theology of his era, not because he knew so little about theology, but because he
knew so much about it. After fifty-five he ceased to
read closely, turned all his theological and philosophical
books over to his brother Edward, went to Dr. Rossiter
W. Raymond for a condensed statement of what was
going on in the realm of science and philosophy, asked
his old friend, Thomas G. Shearman, to do his economic reading for him, and during the last fifteen
years of his life read but few books, and these very
slowly. He left ten thousand volumes, and multitudes
of them never had more than the first fifty leaves cut.
But he was not under the delusion that most of us are
under — that a man has read a book because he owns it.

Some years ago I analyzed Mr. Beecher's published
sermons, and recently I have gone through a large
number of his manuscripts, representing the earlier
period of his ministry. I find that once in three years
he made the round of Christian truth and experience,
preaching on the great epochs of the spiritual life, and
on the great themes, the Scriptures, God, Christ, the
Holy Spirit, man, his dignity, his need, his ignorance
and sinfulness, the nature and number and order of
the spiritual faculties, the method of quickening in
men a sense of sin, the nurture of faith, the development of love, the feeding the hope of the life of
man. But if the themes were many, the ideas that
controlled them were few. No matter what the sub-

ject of the sermon is, during the last thirty years of his preaching four great thoughts dwell in every sermon, as if he had squeezed four clusters of grapes, that the purple flood might run down through all his statements.

The first ruling idea is his conception of the suffering God. For him, God is no "sheaf of thunderstorms." God loves, he pities, he recovers, he sympathizes, he suffers. The very heart of his message is that God neither slumbers nor sleeps, by reason of the emotions of love that suffer and make him the burden-bearer of all his children. As Paul met his Master on the way to Damascus; as Luther, climbing the steps of the church in Rome, received the revelation that he could enter immediately into the presence of God and be saved, so Mr. Beecher, kneeling in the edge of the forest in Indiana, discovered in his vision hour the suffering love of God. For the next forty years that was his one message, and with ever-increasing joy he preached it to the very last hour of his life. From the old pagan notion that was still taught when I was in the seminary, that God was not susceptible to pain, that God dwells at a far remove from this earth, impassive and with marble heart, that God is eternally young and eternally happy, lifted up above all possibility of tears, or anxiety, or solicitude — from all these Grecian and heathen and former ultra-Presbyterian and medieval conceptions he utterly revolted.

Denying that God suffers through any weakness or sin of his own, as man suffers, Mr. Beecher believed that God, as a Father, takes upon himself the sorrows, sufferings and sins of his children. Because he is a Father, because nothing that concerns his children is foreign to him, he suffers with his children's sorrows, and sympathizes in their griefs, and pities those who fear him.   Jesus was filled with compassion when he saw the publican, the prodigal and sinner.   His whole being went out in tides of sympathy toward those who through error or sin had blotted out all the hopes and prophecies of their youth; and if Christ suffered with men through thirty years, God suffers through all the ages and for all the multitudes.   Looking out upon the great pilgrim band journeying across the desert, and blundering as they journeyed, a band struggling, wandering from the way, oft falling in the desert, full oft stricken down by the beasts of passion, sometimes left weltering in their own blood, it seemed to Mr. Beecher impossible for any Christian man to believe that God from his throne in the sky beheld this pilgrim host with any save emotions of sympathy and sorrow and suffering and medicinal love.

About 1870 the scientists began to name God force, and explained the universe by spelling force with a capital "F."   They made God control the world through tides and rivers and winds, so that he had no more personal relation to his universe than the mill stream has to the wheel that grinds the flour. Others represented God as a kind of householder, who built a house, cared for the roof, saw that it was well lighted through the windows, well provisioned as to root cellar and pantry, but who never permitted any one of his children living in the house to know the Father, and himself had no interest in the welfare of his children.   Over against these views Mr. Beecher

unveiled God as the God of suffering love, whose
solicitude for his children burns day and night; God
who cares for all created things, who loves birds, and
cares for the insect in the grass, who loves things

Dr. Lyman Beecher, H. W. Beecher and Harriet Beecher Stowe

empty and crude, things unlovely and seminal, who
loves men who are unlovely and ignorant and sinful,
and who loves, expecting nothing in return. This
all-suffering and all-helpful God is abroad upon a mission of recovery. As the suffering God, he has set

before himself the task of bringing the lowest and
weakest and worst from littleness to largeness, from
ignorance to wisdom, from crudeness and hate to
ripeness and love. The image of his impartial, all-
including, disinterested love is the sun that shines
for the evil and the good. To the last, the sun was
Mr. Beecher's favorite image of the great suffering
God, whose mighty and majestic heart pulsates through
all the universe the tides of his all-cleansing, all-
medicinal, all-forgiving and all-healing love. In scores
of sermons Mr. Beecher never mentions this thought
of the suffering God, and yet, no matter what the
theme is, this thought dwells within and above the
sermon, as the sky overarches the meadows and
orchards with their various grains and fruits.

The second ruling idea of Mr. Beecher was his
conception of the divinity of Jesus Christ. Here he
was an open and self-confessed heretic. In the strict-
est sense he was Sabellian. He did not believe that
Christ had a human intellect or a human will. He
believed that that sacred and divine form that walked
over the hills of Palestine was the luminous point
where God, the creator and sustainer of the universe,
manifested himself. He does indeed manifest himself
through storms that reveal his omnipotence, through
harvests that reveal his goodness, but he also reveals
his love and suffering heart in that human face — the
face of Jesus Christ. It was this conception of Jesus
that in turn gave him his conception of God as the
suffering God of love.

Out of this conception, also, grew his sermon on
the Trinity, in which he argued against the unitary

God, and proclaimed the social nature of God, and
spoke of the assembling of faculties and affections, as
many organs are assembled in one body, and many
faculties in one mind. The Jesus that he preached
was to him the God that he loved. In the same
prayer, therefore, he addresses Jesus and God, his
Father. His one passion was this passion for Jesus
Christ. No one who ever heard Mr. Beecher pray
in the closing years of his life but was impressed with
the way in which he pronounced the words " Jesus "
and " Christ " — for him they were love-words, per-
fumed with the most sacred memories. This conception of Jesus colored all his sermons, even when he
did not refer to it, and was stamped upon even his
philosophical discussions and national themes, as the
king's image is stamped upon gold.

Two other ideas ruled, permeated and colored
Mr. Beecher's sermons, and once a man has found
out what they are he has the key that, with the other
two words, unlocks all the mystery of his discourses;
these two words are the sanctity of the individual and
the certainty of the soul's immortality. Mr. Beecher
held that he was to give an account unto God for himself. Therefore he stood on his own feet, thought his
own thoughts, reached his own conclusions and published them. But he insisted just as earnestly upon
the sacred rights of others. The one striking characteristic of Plymouth Church is the outstanding strength
of its individual men. I can tell a Beecher-grown man
as I can tell a pasture-grown oak. Nothing pleased
Mr. Beecher more than to have his men stand up in
the Friday evening meeting and combat him. He

Plymouth Church, Brooklyn

found therein the proof of his ministry. For that
reason he fed the life of the church spiritually, but
he would not choose its officials. He insisted that
the spiritual life of the church should express itself
by governing itself. His favorite sentence was that
"the poorest government of a church that is self-
government is better than the best government that
I as pastor impose upon them."

But to this overruling idea of the sacredness of
the individual we must add Mr. Beecher's idea of
man's immortality. Looking out upon his vast congregation that crowded aisles and walls, to the
number of nearly three thousand, he saw them all
clothed, not simply with imperfection and knowledge,
with mingled passions and virtues, with hopes and
fears and loves, not simply as pilgrims famished and
hungry, but he also saw them as the children of God,
big with destiny and immortality. This thought of
the immortal life filled him with solemnity. It lent
exhilaration to his reason. It fell like golden sun-
light upon the heads of his congregation. It seemed
like the wistful smile of God. It overflowed his eyes
with tears and his heart with sympathy. It filled his
words with the sweetness of love. He saw that immortal life overarching men as the sky overhangs the
flowers, filling them with rain and dew. For him
what value did this lend to man's soul! What importance did it lend to his sermon! Indeed, the hour
and the sermon, in view of this immortal life, seemed
for the time to Mr. Beecher the only things worth
while. Among his hundreds of sermons, therefore,
with their many messages and their diverse meanings,

there are four all-controlling ideas — the suffering love
of God, the divine Christ, the sacredness of the individual soul, and the certainty of the life immortal.
Having chosen his theme, Mr. Beecher poured the
meanings of these four truths through whatsoever
sermon in such a way as to " convince the man of his
sin, to convert him from his sin and develop in him
the faith of God and the love of Christ, and build up
in him a character after Christ's divine pattern."

Henry Ward Beecher and Harriet Beecher Stowe

HENRY WARD BEECHER AS AN ORATOR

By Rev. Frank W. Gunsaulus, D.D.

No one ever spent a day with Mr. Beecher who did not discern the reason why he was never spoken of by his acquaintances as either a silver- or golden-tongued orator. It is not to disparage Guthrie or Chrysostom that each bears one of these appellations; but it is to indicate the wholeness and integral character of Beecher that his eloquence must be spoken of as an effluence of his entire nature rather than the superb activity of some particular power.

PHYSICAL BASIS OF HIS ORATORY

My study of him as both an organism and an organ commenced shortly after I had read a stimulating and thoughtful production on "The Physical Basis of Oratory." In later years I called up the sagacious remarks in that essay when I saw Gladstone under nearly similar circumstances. In both of these cases one was tempted to ask which had the most influence upon the other, body or mind? Certainly, in the full glow of his creative activity and its expression, each of these men could not have appeared in more characteristic and obedient physical form. Mr. Gladstone's body gave one the conviction that there was more of character in him vertically; Mr. Beecher's that there was more of character in him laterally. Mr. Beecher

swept things with a breadth of mental vision and con-
quest before whose advance an unparalleled variety
of wrongs went down and an equal variety of rights
rejoiced in the fresh revelation of their strength;
Mr. Gladstone illuminated and commanded things by
a height of outlook and insistence under which everything base made a deeper shadow and everything
essentially true rose into sublimer proportions. This,
indeed, is one of the things which the great orator
must do, either through his body or in spite of his
body — he must create an atmosphere in which justice
seems awfully grand and in which injustice seems as
despicable.

It would not be adequate to say that Beecher's
body, at the incandescent moment of his supreme
utterance, was "the organ of his mind." The whole
being called Beecher was organism; he was it and it
was he. If there had not been such integrity, physical
and spiritual, in the fact called Beecher, there would
have been too much of his somewhat too short body.
In Gladstone's case, as I heard him at Liverpool, I
thought if he had spoken with less loftiness and had
avoided what a friend near me called his ingrained
moral narrowness, he would have been just a little too
tall. Such is the miracle of the relationship of mind
and body in the case of the great orator. Of all orators I have ever studied, these men most illustrated
the difference between mind embodied and mind
incarnate.

How much of the effect for brotherly winning and
uplifting toward the apparently cold heights of right-
eousness lay in Beecher's indubitable physical vitality

and his making it a radiation of his spiritual self, I never was quite able to make out. This is probably not oratory but it is of oratory, and without Mr. Beecher's phenomenal power in this respect he could not have won men. Preaching once in Chicago and urging men to climb up by the grace of God from the animal toward the angel, he stood for a moment so excellent an animal as he pronounced the word "basilar" that a base man sitting next to a refined gentleman said: "That man can make me feel that I can be as noble as he looks, when he looks his best, because he gets hold of me physically. He is the real thing in both cases." This is character rather than oratory obeying what is called "the first principles of address in starting from the level of ordinary thought and feeling."

Nevertheless it is oratory, too. If he had not opened his mouth, the impression would have been that made by an orator, the orator being, as Fox said, "one who can give immediate instantaneous utterance to his thoughts." Eloquence is always more than one says; it is the communication of what one is at his best. John Bright and Henry Ward Beecher had massive proportions to the eye, like Burke and Fox, Webster and Chalmers, but the study of all these will not disclose such an interesting likeness as that which abides between Beecher and Mirabeau. Every man has his rhythm, just as every man has his body; the rhythm and the stout, elastic frame of either of these men, differing startlingly as they do, might be taken for those of the other.

HIS SERENITY

Mr. Beecher's incandescence was not less impressive because he was not always incandescent. He
could literally withdraw himself from the front door
or windows of his house and be somnolent, or go into
one of the chambers of himself and take a nap mentally. I have seen him doing this with his eyes wide
open ; others were suffering from the irritating prose
of a would-be poet-speaker ; he was simply withdrawn
into the cushioned serenity of himself. It was on the
occasion of the Herbert Spencer banquet ; and eminent but very heavy were some of the speakers.
Spencer looked at times as if he wished he had not
written the books which they praised. More than one
distinguished man looked tired and bored.

Shortly before Beecher was called upon, the refreshed soul which had now forsaken its couch, where
it had been safe from the irritation of illustrious dull-
ness, came forth and looked out through the windows
— those eyes of unforgetable lucidity and depth. All
of him spoke from the instant he found his feet beneath him. Mentally alert and entirely furnished with
knowledge, he was more distinguished in that speech
through the luminosity of his moral attributes. It
was the most courageous speech I had heard from
Mr. Beecher.

HIS FEARLESSNESS

My father had repeated to my childhood passages
from addresses which he had heard Mr. Beecher
deliver when mobs were howling about him and he
confronted the horrible visage of Civil War; and

Interior of Plymouth Church in Mr. Beecher's day

he always told me that Mr. Beecher impressed him
as fearful, yea, decidedly afraid of two things — the
possibility of being wrong mentally with respect to
the subject he was talking about, and the moral peril
of being unwilling to stand by the truth as he saw it
and be its champion to the end. His whole soul was
so intent with this wholesome fear that he had no
other. He was like Lord Lawrence, who "feared
God so much that he feared not man at all." On
that occasion he was not delighting Herbert Spencer
with his discriminating and warm eulogy; he was
courageously paying a debt of gratitude and discharg-
ing an obligation with utmost freedom, but every
attitude uttered Paul's words, "With a great sum
have I obtained this freedom."

Such eloquence as Mr. Beecher's is impossible
without that courage which invigorates the brain and
makes the will resistless. It may be born and nursed
in the heart and enswathed in the emotions, as the
term suggests, but it alone rescues a man from frag-
mentariness and makes him whole and holy as a leader
of men through public speech. Intellect, sensibilities
and will are not separate compartments, but constitute
one overflowing cup of power in all eloquence.

Doubtless those of us who were too young to have
beheld the monarch when he was a war-horse "and his
neck was clothed with thunder," received the somewhat similar impression of the vivifying and unifying
influence of his courage as an oratorical force when we
heard him in the times of his severest trial. Was it a
lecture on preaching which had taken shape as the
bitter cup was pressed to his lips, or a lecture given

in a strange town after a throng of hoodlums had be-
fouled the air with their vile hooting, or a sermon to
college young men such as I heard within an hour
after he had been made aware of the dreadful avalanche which was approaching him, he was the same
fervent, human unit throughout the illuminating hour.
In those times the effect upon a discriminating hearer
was that of a total character — a character totalized by
fiery courage, making his eloquence opalescent because
its fire was revealed everywhere.

HIS SELF—CONTROL

If Mr. Beecher had not possessed a magnetic
centralness of character which forbade easily sepa-
rable powers and interests from straying out the field,
he would have been simply the most multitudinous
collection of forces which ever failed in public life.
He had wit and humor; almost always they did not
have him. To change the figure, he would strike a
vein which, if followed up, would have made him a
clown tossing grotesque chunks of ore as no Grimaldi
might have done; but suddenly the swirling fires of
his persistent purpose in speech would melt the ore
and the fine gold would be coined into noble thoughts.
His humor would often bubble forth with a hint that
the hearer might soon be overwhelmed, but inimitably
the master of himself was its master, and a cup full
of sparkling water would be handed to one whose
throat had been a little dry and whose appetite now
was ready for wisdom.

With an art for epigram he surprised his audience,
but never lost them or left them standing at the quick

turn in the roadway where so unexpectedly came the
brief and brilliant vision.   The temptation to let the
wheels of the mind go round, because the machinery
was noiseless, had its death at birth in the fact that
anything like conceit over such a happy state of things

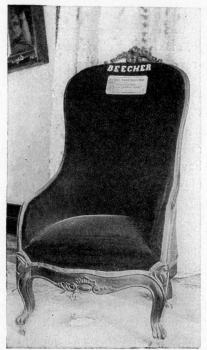

Chair used by Mr. Beecher in Plymouth Pulpit

was lost in the serious purpose of his address, which
was to make others think and feel and will as he did.
As much might be said of his boundless sympathy.
Those eyes were roguish with laughter no more often
than they were wet with tears.   At the old Soldiers'

Home in Dayton, Ohio, I saw him touch a flag and heard him utter a sentence with the result that everybody was weeping and he himself was almost unmanned with emotion. Instantly the disorganized man was reorganized by that centralizing life purpose which permitted no waste of such precious energies. He saw his relationship to future problems, and realized that only a stern devotion to duty and the highest wisdom could meet those issues. It is this forceful manhood, permeated with loyalty to God and man, which must ever be regarded as the energizing and saving secret of Beecher the orator.

HIS VOICE

So far as the art of the orator is concerned, Mr. Beecher's voice, which is but the string upon the instrument, was the organ of the organism most apparently in evidence. Like a violinist of the highest power, when he touched it his total self touched it. He could play an excellent tune, like Paganini, on one string, but any such consideration of the stringed instrument overestimates the string; it must not leave out the instrument especially.

No elocutionary training could have saved him from ministerial sore throat, or his audience from ministerial sore ears, which is a consequential and not less distressing malady. His justness of emphasis came from his fine perception; his painter-like sympathy for rightness of color, and his will to express himself in perfect draughtsmanship — simply to transfer his character into another character, was the supreme and easy task to which he called his voice. To tell the truth as he saw it required an instrument unabused by vociferation and free from the sharpness which comes from saying sharp things too frequently, which often cuts the thread of truth. It must indeed be entirely melodious as truth itself is. There was spiritual good breeding in Beecher's tones. Such a voice cannot be made in one generation. It was as variable as the portraits of the man, yet from thunder to whisper it was Beecher's voice.

This artistic passion was allied with almost un-erring artistic wisdom. Like George Inness, whose paintings are a revelation of the gradual evolution of a soul Mr. Beecher was one of the first to understand, the great preacher himself advanced from an almost pharisaic legalism to an almost unparalleled liberty. He knew the secret of elimination. "Thou canst if thou wilt" — so the devil always says to a big, brainy and capable man. Animated and ardent, the orator always feels as Webster did when, after talking a few moments in reply to Hayne, everything that he had ever thought or heard or read was within his grasp, and he had only "to seize a thunderbolt as it went smoking by and hurl it at him."

More than thunderbolts came into the field of Beecher's vision, urging themselves on his attention and pleading to enter into his picture, but he had the ability to leave this pretty flower and that noble tree out of his canvas. "This one thing I do" — that was the intensely wrought law, self-imposed and radiant, to which he gave obedience. So will the artist live for-ever in his art, as Raphael in his Sistine Madonna and Richard Wagner in Parsifal.

AN ENGLISH ESTIMATE OF BEECHER

By Rev. W. J. Dawson, D.D.

The Minister of Highbury Quadrant Congregational Church, London.

Henry Ward Beecher is for many of us in England the greatest preacher of the last decades of the nineteenth century. Spurgeon surpassed him in evangelical force, Liddon in the elaboration of his rhetoric, Parker in brilliancy of phrase, but none of these equaled him in general mass of intellect, in philosophic grasp, in native genius. It is hard to say what genius is; we endeavor to define it by such terms as charm, magnetism, and a peculiar lambency of mind, "a light that never was on sea or land"; but whatever it is, no one could be in Beecher's company for half an hour without knowing that he possessed it. He had in a supreme degree the "genius to be loved." He captivated men without an effort. He never attempted to do anything that could be called great, and yet he was always great. He appeared absolutely simple, and yet his simplicity was the last equation of profundity. He was a preacher by vocation, but he made one feel that he could as easily have been a statesman, a prime minister, or the president of a republic. It is scarcely an exaggeration to say that while Beecher lived no other American bulked very large in English eyes. He was the typical American of his generation. He rose so high, he cast so large a shadow, he held the gaze so completely, that when we English folk thought of America we always thought of Beecher. To us he seemed the incarnation of the national genius.

The salient quality which impressed me most in Beecher was the supreme ease with which he did his work. I had not the good fortune to meet him on his historic visit to England in the sixties; that was before my time. During his last visit to England, however, I heard him often; I sat beside him on the platform; I had ample opportunity of studying his methods of address; and this supreme ease with which he did his work filled me with astonishment. He never seemed agitated, nervous, or conscious of the least strain, however vast the congregation he addressed. His audiences were not always quite friendly. There was an undercurrent of suspicion which he was much too sensitive not to perceive. But he moved before these vast crowds always like a man at ease. He knew his own integrity and he knew his own power. The moment he began to speak the spell of his personality began to work.

PECULIARITY OF HIS ORATORY

At first his speaking created a sense of disappointment; it was so quiet, so colloquial, so free from the usual artifice of the orator. He seemed to be standing at a height, aloof from his audience, talking to himself of things which were of moment to himself alone. He did not even try to make himself heard, and many amusing contests of wit between himself and his hearers arose on this matter. "Can't hear," shouted out a man in a raucous voice in Exeter Hall

Mrs. Beecher

one night. "I never meant you to hear that,"
Beecher retorted, and calmly pursued the course of
his argument. Men looked at one another and mutely
asked what they had come out for to see. Where were
the brilliant paradox, the flash of epigram, the sono-
rous declamation which English audiences had learned
to expect from their popular orators? Where were the
passion and intensity which lift an audience to its
feet? Men remembered John B. Gough, and won-
dered at Beecher's reputation. They remembered
the full roll of Bright's and Gladstone's eloquence,
stately, impressive, full of magnificent modulations,
an eloquence like the sound of many waters.

This quiet man went on talking with himself. It
seemed to him of no importance whether his audience
thought well or ill of him. Then, suddenly, he emitted
a spark of flame that ran kindling through the crowd.
He said something so daring or so piquant that men
began to sit up stiff upon their seats and lean forward
in anxious listening. There came a flash of humor,
a touch of pathos, and the audience quivered; a
moment later frantic excitement seized upon the congregation. And still he was talking with the utmost
quietness, complete master of himself as well as of
his hearers. It was a new kind of oratory. Nothing
had been heard like it in England, and nothing has
been heard since. So Coleridge might have talked
out of the depth of an experience and wisdom that
seemed more than finite — the old man eloquent. It
was a kind of oratory almost too rare to be called
oratory. It was in truth much more than oratory; it
was the speech of the soul finding by unerring instinct

its way to the deepest springs of life and thought in
his hearers.   .

GREATER THAN HIS WORK

There is a useful distinction which I have often
had occasion to draw between writers and speakers
who seem more than their works and those who seem
less. In reading some books and listening to some
men I am conscious that the best, and even more than
the best, that is in them has found adequate expression. They have gained a height, but it has been at
the expenditure of the last ounce of strength. With
Beecher I felt precisely the reverse. There were
reserves in him which he never called into action.
He drew upon a mind so full, a nature so rich that
he had no need to husband his resources. His personality exceeded by far his finest effort to express it.
He could afford to be lavish ; he could always have
done better than his best if he had so willed it. Very
few men produce this impression.

George Meredith impresses me and all who know
him as being much greater than his works. Coleridge
impressed his contemporaries as greater than his
poetry. There is a kind of divine carelessness in
Shakespeare ; he is a giant who never used his
strength to the full. Beecher, also, I think, stands
in this rare category. Nothing that he did was so
great as himself. No sermon he preached and no
book which he has left behind him gives us anything
like an adequate measurement of his genius. There
was a kind of primeval depth and freshness in him ;
he was inexhaustible as nature herself. In this re-

[3d poster ; size, 25x38 inches.]

WHO IS

HY. WARD BEECHER?

He is the man who said the best blood of England must be shed to atone for the *Trent* affair.

He is the man who advocates a War of Extermination with the South,—says it is incapable of "re-generation," but proposes to re-people it from the North by "generation."—See "Times."

He is the friend of that inhuman monster, General BUTLER. He is the friend of that so-called Gospel Preacher, CHEEVER, who said in one of his sermons—"Fight against the South till *Hell* Freezes, and then continue the battle on the ice."

He is the friend and supporter of a most debased Female, who uttered at a public meeting in America the most indecent and cruel language that ever polluted female lips.—See "Times."

MEN OF MANCHESTER, ENGLISHMEN!

What reception can you give this wretch, save unmitigated disgust and contempt? His impudence in coming here is only equalled by his cruelty and impiety Should he, however, venture to appear, it behooves all right-minded men to render as futile as the first this second attempt to get up a public demonstration in favor of the North, which is now waging War against the South with a vindictive and revengeful cruelty unparalleled in the history of any Christian land.

English Poster of 1863

spect Beecher is unique. I have heard many sermons and addresses more brilliant than anything which I heard from him ; I have never met a man who gave me such a sense of inexhaustible depth of nature.

FAREWELL MEETING AT CITY TEMPLE

The most triumphant display of ability which I have ever known was Beecher's farewell meeting at the City Temple, on his last visit. He spoke all together for about two hours and a half. I sat beside him, and was amazed to find that the entire notes for his address did not fill half a sheet of note-paper. Never was his humor fresher, never was he more tender and wise than in that address. But remark-

able as the address was, it was insignificant beside
what followed. He offered to answer questions on
any subjects which the audience might select. The
subjects selected were as wide as human thought.
They ranged from the nature of the Trinity to the
ethics of socialism. They included anxious questions
about eternal punishment and absurd questions about
Anglican orders.

Never once did Beecher falter. His adroitness,
his nimbleness of mind, his wit, his keen penetration
into the characters of his questioners, were simply
astounding. It was only sheer hunger and exigency
of time that broke up the meeting. The people would
have remained for hours longer, and Beecher showed
no trace of weariness. Indeed, he humorously com-
plained, when Dr. Parker closed the meeting, that he
was beginning to enjoy himself. Those who heard
Beecher on that memorable morning knew how true
it was that the man was infinitely greater than his
works. They witnessed the free, untrammeled display
of a supreme genius using every means of expression
with equal ease, capable of rising to any demands
made upon it, moving with a kind of effortless felicity
through the loftiest realms of human thought ; and
great and admirable as were some of the men ranged
round Beecher that day, they and the audience alike
felt that no one of them approached that solitary
greatness which distinguished Beecher.

MORE THAN A RHETORICIAN

Beecher taught the preachers of England many
great lessons, and their debt to him is incalculable.

He taught us naturalness. He taught us the value
of speech as distinguished from mere oratory. He
showed us how great was the power of the man
who could think upon his feet. He taught us that
neither claptrap nor highly-wrought artificial rhetoric,
nor even a popular theme, was needed to win the
ear of the listening multitude. Given the man who
thought clearly, who felt deeply, who spoke out of
his heart in good, honest vernacular, and there was
no theme, however philosophic, that could not engage
the deepest interest of an audience. We needed those
lessons, for the traditions of pulpit eloquence when
Beecher began his ministry were mostly of a quite
different kind. I do not wish to speak a single
disparaging word of such genuine pulpit orators as
Parsons, of York, or Morley Punshon, but we know
that their eloquence was artificial in form, the result
of laborious elaboration, built up upon deliberate an-
tithesis and climax and crowned with glittering perora-
tions. Spurgeon had already struck a hard blow at
this method of preaching, but it needed a Beecher to
demolish it. It needed some one to show us that the
freedom of plain speech was not only suited to simple
evangelical appeals, but also to the widest ranges of
philosophic thought.

To have heard Beecher was an era in the life of
many a young preacher. He went home to prepare
himself instead of his sermons. He saw that the
secret of pulpit force was in direct talk, as between
man and man. He saw that to be himself was a
better aim than to imitate any one else, however
worthy of imitation. He discovered that the full

mind, the big heart, the intense soul, made the successful preacher — these, and these alone. That was a great lesson to learn. It revolutionized the pulpit, and to this day the English pulpit bears the mark of Beecher, and has cause to thank him.

REV. H. W. BEECHER'S
MISSION TO LIVERPOOL.
THE TRENT AFFAIR.

[Rev. H. W BEECHER in the *New York Independent*.]

"Should the President quietly yield to the present necessity (viz.. the delivering up of Messrs. Mason and Slidell) as the lesser of two evils and bide our time with England, there will be a

SENSE of WRONG, of NATIONAL HUMILIATION
SO PROFOUND, AND A
HORROR OF THE UNFEELING SELFISHNESS OF THE ENGLISH GOVERNMENT

in the great emergency of our affairs, such as will inevitably break out by and by in flames, and which will only be extinguished by a deluge of blood! We are not living the whole of our life to-day. There is a future to the United States in which the nation will right any injustice of the present hour."

The Rev. Henry Ward Beecher, at a meeting held in New York, at the time when the Confederate Envoys, Messrs. Slidell and Mason, had been surrendered by President Lincoln to the British Government, from whose vessel (the Royal Mail Steamer *Trent*) they were taken, said

"That the Best Blood of England must flow for the outrage England had perpetrated on America."

This opinion of a Christian (?) minister, wishing to obtain a welcome in Liverpool, whose operatives are suffering almost unprecedented hardships, caused by the suicidal war raging in the States of North America, and urged on by the fanatical Statesmen and Preachers of the North, is worthy of consideration.

Poster displayed in England when Mr. Beecher spoke there in 1863

INFLUENCE ON THEOLOGY

And Beecher did even more to revolutionize our theology. He would probably have disowned the claim to be a theologian ; he was rather a humanist than a theologian, yet his influence on theology was great. He helped to deliver us from barbaric formulæ ; he made us conscious of the magnanimity of God. For myself, I bless his memory. He was one of the greatest and one of the best of men. The further we remove from him in time the more clearly do we see the dimension of his genius. I believe that America has produced no greater man, that the pulpit has boasted no more fruitful force. No homage done to his memory can be extravagant, and I rejoice, in the name of multitudes of my countrymen, to lay this humble wreath of praise upon his honored grave.

MR. BEECHER AS AUTHOR AND EDITOR

By John R. Howard

In December, 1867, Mr. Beecher entered into contract with the publishing firm of J. B. Ford and Company to write "The Life of Jesus, the Christ"; and the undertaking was an intimate part of his life until he died, in 1887. Indeed, it was about the latest subject of his thought; the day before his fatal attack he asked me to meet him the next evening with reference to the renewal of his work upon it. From the outset it meant much to him: it formed the basis of his studies; it gave fresh inspiration to his pulpit effort and enrichment to his thought, and was at once the stimulus and the conservative check in his use of the new evolutionary philosophy, which was gradually changing his views of things human and divine.

This and the other publications that rapidly ensued — Plymouth Pulpit, The Christian Union, and the issue of volumes of sermons, lectures, and other matters new and renewed (altogether about forty volumes) — entailed upon the members of the firm a familiarity with his ways of working. One can hardly speak of his "methods," since the exigencies of his life precluded him from system — except as to sermon-making and preaching, always his main business.

Yet he worked on general principles, too. "Reading maketh a full man;" and this man's habit of reading — not in preparation for specific productions

57

so much as for broad comprehension of departments
and phases of thought — furnished his mind and stimulated its powers. Witness in early manhood his
Indianapolis experiences. When at one time he had
continued daily preaching during eighteen consecutive
months, for relaxation after preaching he took up the
Loudon encyclopædias — of horticulture, agriculture
and architecture; also Lindley's "Horticulture" and
Gray's "Structural Botany"; all of which he says he
read, "not only every line, but much of it many times
over." Thus he confirmed his original love of nature
and acquired an understanding of it, so that his
much-praised work, when shortly after he edited The
Western Farmer and Gardener, was out of well-earned
knowledge.

Most of Mr. Beecher's books were but the print-
ing of his spoken words; "Norwood," and "The Life
of Jesus, the Christ," together with sundry volumes of
"Star Papers," etc., are exceptions. The first is a
charming series of chapters on New England scenery
and life, with enough of a story to hold it together,
and more wit, wisdom, philosophy and religion than
often get into a "novel." This required no study of
material, but was a weary labor of pen-work to his
unaccustomed hand. The "Life" is a most luminous
and suggestive exposition of the deeds and words of
the Master.

The work on the Life of Christ was begun in a
fashion like his early horticultural studies. He had
already kept well abreast with the orthodox and the
skeptical schools of England, France and Germany,
while maintaining interest in the new lines of the

evolutionary writers, but now undertook to familiarize himself thoroughly with them. He welcomed these varied lights of criticism and philosophy; yet he recognized what he called "the chill mist of doubt" arising from them, while his spiritual nature craved and held to the truths of the other world; so that he took the materials of the Gospels as his final and unquestioned basis. Moreover, he felt that too many of the attempts to write the Life of Christ had been dialectical and critical in spirit, and, as he wrote, "while they may lead scholars from doubt into certainty, they are likely to lead plain people from certainty into doubt, and to leave them there. I have, therefore," he continued, "studiously avoided a polemic spirit, seeking to produce conviction without controversy."

While carefully considering the works of critical objectors, then, he did not argue against them, but endeavored, as far as possible, so to state the facts as to take away the grounds from which the objections were aimed; in brief, to depict not the modern subject of discussions, but the Jesus of the four Evangelists, in his disposition, his social relations, his deeds and his doctrines.

But all this laying out of the ground took time, and he wrote but little for a year or two. The first volume, however, was published in June, 1871, and in 1872–3 he had written about two-thirds of the second; after that, nothing.

In discussing Mr. Beecher as author and editor some drawbacks to his performance of pen-duties must be noted. First, there was his great church.

Such cares as this entailed, together with his preaching and lecture-room services, were his chief interest
at all times. Besides this, there were the incessant
demands upon him from the public to be the voice on
all important occasions ; there were interviews with
reporters, and such a multiplicity of applications for
sympathy and aid from citizens beyond his parish and
from strangers as probably few men have ever been
subject to.

There were other — at first subtle, and afterwards
outbreaking and volcanic — obstructions to the equabil-
ity of mind needed for such work. These are familiar,
and need not be rehearsed, but enough has been suggested to show how impossible it was for Mr. Beecher
to have regular methods of literary labor. He had to
work as he could, and, lacking the habit of system,
he was obliged to await the mood. When it came, his
quill flew over the paper with impatient leaps and
dashes, and he produced very rapidly.

Perhaps a reminiscence, which I find in an old
journal of mine kept at that time, will give a clear
idea of his way of working as author. After the
completion of Volume I of this book, in June, 1871,
he meant, after the summer's rest, to go right on
into Volume II ; but in January, 1872, he commenced
the first of his three series of " Lectures on Preaching"
before the Yale Divinity School, so that he did very
little writing — on the book, none. He was reading,
however. One day I went in and found him deep in
a book, before the fire. " I'm reading up on miracles,"
he cried, with a kind of glee ; " I feel the swellings
of new buds ; I shall have to begin again soon ! "

But he did not. On April 29 I said to him, "Do
you know that March 1st is gone, and April 1st is
gone, and May 1st is at hand, and that new writing
is not even *begun?*" "I do, to my sorrow," he answered. "And to-morrow, unless the Lord hates me,
I shall begin upon it."

So the next morning, when I called in, he was up
in his study. He had his "Volume I" before him,

The Hicks Street house in which Mr. Beecher died

his "Consolidated Gospels," and a clean lot of paper.
"The next thing," said he, "is the Gadarenes and
the pigs," and he gave a funny snuffle. "I don't
know exactly how to treat that episode. If I come
at it from the critical and explanatory side, I invite
attack from all quarters — for I can't agree with
everybody, and as to fighting in this book, I *won't!*
There is a graphic and dramatic way of treating all
these strange and miraculous elements, as Shakespeare treated the supernatural — using it for his pur-

pose, but leaving it without an attempt to explain or
make it intelligibly real. In fact, these things occur
in the New Testament history in much that way.
They come quietly into view, like a cloud — which
looms up, casts its shadow on the landscape for a
time, and passes away without effort or commotion.
Treated thus, they offend no darling theory ; no critic
is agitated to attack the view, and the moral and
spiritual effect aimed at is achieved. I don't know
what the critics *would* have done with my book without that chapter on 'The Doctrinal Basis.' That
seems their only hold ; to all the rest they are mild
as milk. After all, this attempting to theologize on
God and his manifestation in Jesus is but the meager-
est and poorest way of getting at him. The theory —
any theory of that problem — never made a man a
Christian yet ; but the simple statement that God so
loved the world that he sent his own Son to die for
it, that is intelligible to the heart of man. It is at
once a force, a motive. The attempt to commute a
moral impulse into an intellectual idea is about like
changing grapes into wine. The wine is good for
some purposes, undoubtedly, but it isn't *grapes* — the
form is changed and it becomes an entirely different
thing."

And, in fact, that single chapter was the only
portion objected to by anybody ; it was theological,
and that was enough to invite dissent. The volume
stands to-day a fit memorial of the intellectual and
spiritual nature of the man ; a treasury of noble
thoughts, of delicate imaginings, of stimulating suggestions, shrewd readings of human nature, a pro-

found insight into the character of Jesus. It is a
great example of Mr. Beecher's wonderfully combined
common sense and lofty spirituality.

After some more talking about the topic in hand,
he said, "Well, now you shall see me begin Volume
Second," and with his spattering quill he dashed off
the title of the next chapter.

He had two "good days," and when I saw him on
the evening of the second, he said, "I had expected
to have a severe tussle with those maniacs and devils
among the Gadarenes, but I think I've finished them;
another such day and I'll have finished my chapter."

I mentioned a certain book we had been discussing previously, and asked if he found it of any special
use. "No," he replied, "I find no single book help-
ful when I am actively at work. I do not generally
like to read studiously any one book when I am
writing. I am very sensitive to books, and do not
wish to get myself impressed in any given direction.
I prefer to take up one after another, especially books
of original investigation, and get the general effect of
their views. Thus I am able to form my own opinion
under the cross-lights of all these others, and the result is that my way of stating it, when completed, is
more likely to be true and less likely to be offensive
to any. I try to find the elements of truth in each,
and so to get a many-sided view."

I find among my fragmentary memoranda of those
days one dated "Christmas, 1874," which gives one
of his suggestive ways of looking at the familiar
gospel story, which I do not believe he ever put
upon paper. He said:

"I have just been planning out a new chapter."
With the publisher's instinct, I asked, "Did you jot
it down?" "No; it is a very clear line of thought.
It is the development of contrast between the appar-
ent literalness and the real mysticism of Christ's
teachings. All through his life and sayings ran a
double line. He, himself, knew it and avowed it.
He taught them in parables, that hearing they might
not understand; and they felt it, too, for they came
to him and asked, 'How long makest thou us to
doubt?' Now, in view of this, look back at the
Sermon on the Mount. There was proclaimed a line
of ethics in regard to personal morality, to honesty,
to self-defense, etc., that if taken literally would be
utterly subversive of society. See how it comes out
in John's Gospel and grows more and more strong to
the very end! How he plays with the figures of the
vine, the life, the light, bread, wine, mansions, etc.,
flashing them here and there like illusions! He was
the most mystical and figurative of teachers. In face
of this, when people come to some single point, like
the finality of punishment, see how they pin you down
to the literal words given in translation as the words
of Jesus — 'He *said* so and so' — as if he were usually given to saying the exact, literal thing that he
meant!"

During 1872-3 Mr. Beecher wrote seven or eight
chapters of the Second Volume; then other matters
broke in, the building process was stopped, and although he several times tried to start it again —
notably in the last year of his life — the grand work
stands uncompleted, except as it was pieced out, in

Boscobel, Mr. Beecher's house in Peekskill

most interesting fashion, from his sermons, by his
son, William C. Beecher, and his son-in-law, Rev.
Samuel Scoville. And the possibility of that, by the
way, shows how his interests and studies kept him
upon the line of the Master's words and works through
many years.

Despite the fact that Mr. Beecher did a vast
amount of writing, the mechanical effort of putting
pen to paper so lagged behind his thought that it
was a perpetual hindrance and annoyance to him. In
proof-reading, too, he suffered the disadvantage of
having his words come back to him as something
not altogether his own. At the time of utterance,
his thinking pressed for outlet so that he gave little
heed to form. Although the general matter was prepared beforehand, and long habit had given him command of a noble vocabulary and a forceful style, his
plan often changed while he was preaching; its presentation was incited by the moment, and its mode
was in all details a matter of "unconscious cerebra-
tion." It was somewhat so, too, in writing, for he
wrote as he spoke, in heat; and when the material
came before him in cold printer's ink it was, in a
manner, strange to him; so that instead of merely
"correcting," he found stimulus to fresh thinking,
and was apt to make havoc with the printer's work.
All these things hindered him, both in authorship and
in journalistic work. His sermons he rarely saw until
they came to him in the Plymouth Pulpit pamphlet;
he left to others their correcting, a certain rough editing of obvious tongue-slips, and the giving of titles.

Yet, that his discourses were thoroughly planned

Home of Eunice White Bullard, Sutton, Mass.

Photo by G. Butler

was made evident when the manuscript report of one
of his "Yale Lectures on Preaching" had been lost,
and the stenographer had by some fatality mislaid or
destroyed his notes.   Mr. Beecher sat patiently and
reproduced the lecture — of course, not in the original
words, but in the distinct line of thought — while it
was stenographically taken over again for publication.
His ideas were clear to his own mind; when he
changed during preaching, it was because he came
upon something that he considered more important
than his original preparation.   In writing, he did
less of this than most men.   His manuscripts and
proofs of the Life of Christ show many changes of
expression, but not many alterations in the idea he
had chosen to put forward.

One of Mr. Beecher's editorial labors should be
at least mentioned — the "Plymouth Collection of
Hymns and Tunes," the pioneer of Congregational
singing in America, with a word as to its courageous
inclusion, greatly to the enrichment of worship, of
hymns from Catholic, Unitarian and other sources,
then unusual to the orthodox Protestant.

Mr. Beecher's editing of The Christian Union de-
serves more than a final sentence or two.   He had had
experience in journalism.   While a theological student
he had for some months edited The Cincinnati Journal,
in Indianapolis The Western Farmer and Gardener, and
both with noticeable ability.   He had written much for
The New York Independent, with national effect, and
was for some time its editor.   He had his own ideas
about a religious paper, and infused them into The
Christian Union.   He made it purely unsectarian,

although he himself was a sturdy Congregationalist, with firm belief in the independence and the fellowship of the churches. As he announced, he did "breathe, through the columns of The Christian Union, Christian love, courage, equity, and gentleness." He aimed to abolish the "sacred" and "secular" discrimination, and to bring the spirit of Christ to bear upon all the interests of man.

During the first year (1870) he wrote much for the paper (and none on the book); after that he kept his eye, his mind and his heart on the former — and his hand, too — influencing its workers much as he did Plymouth Church. His spirit informed and guided it, and, no less than his name, was the power that swept it to its great success, although ably supplemented by the clear-eyed management and admirable editorial writing of Mr. George S. Merriam, the working editor for five and a half years, who furnished, of course, an indispensable element.

There is no space to detail Mr. Beecher's many peculiarities — of rapid and forceful writing, of either reluctant or destructive and reconstructive proof-reading, the alternations of despair and exaltation among his coworkers at getting nothing from him, or being rejoiced by an article or inspired by an hour of eloquent talk at the office. The field is wide, but this corner of it is fenced in by the limits of a brief article. And here we must leave it.

The memory of the man, in the consciousness of one who knew him intimately for forty years and worked beside him for twenty, is one of boundless mental resource, perennial humor and sunniness of

temper, a profound spirituality, and an amazingly practical embodiment of the spirit of Christ in living goodness.   Here was a sweet-souled, great-hearted, Christian, manly man, a life employed with rare singleness
of purpose in bringing Christ to men and men to
Christ.

THE CONTRIBUTION OF MR. BEECHER TO LITERATURE

By Rev. Alford B. Penniman, Chicago

LOOKING over my large Beecher library I am at a loss to tell what to omit in a relative estimate. Mr. Beecher himself disclaimed rank among men of letters as he disclaimed place among professional theologians. We cannot imagine Mr. Beecher hanging around a country churchyard seven years to produce one poem, as did Gray. He wrote spontaneously out of his mood and vision, as Burns wrote much of "Tam O'Shanter" during a few moments when Jean Armour stole along quietly behind him in the broomcorn on the bank of the Nith. He was a prose poet, endowed for work of the first order. Like his Master, he wrote on the popular heart rather than on parchment. He spoke in parables to the whole man instead of risking content with more limited influence. Literature as the incarnation rather than the dress of thought, he held in high esteem. From this point of view his literary work has been vastly underestimated. His humanism is so unique that his books will abide. The *odium theologicum*, not above bringing to its aid false witness and scandal, has only a little delayed a more just estimate of his literary work.

Even in the chance fragments culled from his sermons he was great. He rose in spite of the

"periodical misreports of the reporters." Many well-
arranged anthologies have appeared. One extensive
selection of five hundred indexed pages was compiled
by Rev. G. D. Evans, of London (1870), and entitled,
"One Thousand Gems," veritable "apples of gold in
pictures of silver." The English publishers have
often been more diligent to gather Mr. Beecher's
sermons and scatter them over the world than have
our own. Mr. Dickinson, of Farringdon Street, London, sold me two volumes entitled, "Forty-eight
Sermons by Henry Ward Beecher, Preached Previous
to 1867." Up to that time, on this side of the sea,
no enterprise corresponds to that period save the
elephantiasis issues of The Independent and some old-
time journals.

About 1867 Dr. Lyman Abbott began a better
selection. From five hundred sermons he, with the
aid of Mr. Beecher, chose forty-six, representing much
variety of theme, construction and treatment. The
next series of sermons is now published in ten volumes under five covers, containing two hundred and
sixty-three sermons. This treasure mine is so much
of it pure gold that no one has proposed to smelt it
over, certainly not into forty-six sermons for this
period between 1869–73.

If a theological student can get only one series
of Mr. Beecher's sermons, his choice should fall upon
the series from 1873–75, being one hundred and four
sermons in four volumes, representing the height of
his personality and pulpit power.

From 1875 on, the authorized publication of his
sermons continued in unabated power, as found in the

weekly issue of Plymouth Pulpit. Special note should be made of the anticipation of the newer Bible study in his " Bible Studies," or the publication of certain Sunday evening lectures. The volume, " Evolution and Religion," dealt with nature, revelation and the background of mystery, and other related themes. It was his last great message to a generation of youth trained in scientific studies or indirectly affected by them. It was the message of a teacher calmly unfolding the results of the long brooding and practical years ; a teacher who taught what he termed a " seminal theory of development" long before the publication of the " Origin of Species."

The best work of Mr. Beecher's life, before, during, or after the war, was done under fire. The " Life of Christ" was written during his trouble of the seventies. Asked why he did not write about the later scenes as well as the earlier in the life of our Lord he replied, " Perhaps God has a Gethsemane for *me* to pass through as a preparation for that work."

Another book indispensable for the young man entering the ministry is the " Yale Lectures on Preaching," delivered in three series from 1872 to 1874. Comparing them with each other, the third series is the best, the first series ranks next and the second series, though valuable, is third in relative importance.

Let us not fail to note how unbiased men, for example, in Great Britain, who knew him almost entirely by his books, regarded him. For this testimony read " A Summer in England with Henry Ward Beecher" (1886), compiled by the late Major James B.

Pond. There are passages in this book, quoted from
Mr. Beecher, which represent a very apotheosis of
friendship, heart power and benediction. Nothing
in the classic memoirs of Charles Kingsley, F. D.
Maurice or Norman Macleod equals them.

The volume entitled "Patriotic Addresses" is his
one book appealing to all sorts of civilized and un-
civilized men. It is an octavo of eight hundred and
fifty-seven pages. Here lives again the victorious
reformer, prophet-statesman and orator, glowing in
cold type, converting the public sentiment of Britain
from hate to neutrality, and finally to friendship with
enthusiasm; raising the flag at Sumter, "without the
loss of a single star"; making himself almost a
necessity to the salvation of this whole brave nation;
affording material for an American epic by an
American Homer, perchance some untrammeled Burns,
whose poetic genius, more likely than not, will find
him in the wilderness, as Lincoln and Beecher were
found.

As the light of day fades on his honest toil his
words ring the *angelus* of a new church catholic, and
chime the chant of faith and hope and love; words
matchless, home-stained, radiant, condensed, sunbeams
burning and beautiful; words of our great friend and
commoner, the minister of racial brotherhood and
divine love, Henry Ward Beecher.

AN ABRIDGED BEECHER BIBLIOGRAPHY

SUPPLEMENTARY TO BOOKS MENTIONED IN FOREGOING
ARTICLE. — A. B. P.

1. THE *Seven Lectures to Young Men* delivered at Indianapolis is the "eldest born" of Mr. Beecher's books (1844). To this volume were added five more lectures of the same period. D. Appleton and Company, 1879, is the copyright mark of my copy. This is written in his early tropical style, but not overdrawn for life in the West at that time. When Dr. James Brand, of Oberlin, applied in a sermon the personification of the "corrupter of youth" (page 187) to one Thad. Rowland, reputed as a masked saloon-keeper of a drug-store in Oberlin, there was enough ginger left in the lecture on Popular Amusements to result in Dr. Brand being sued for two thousand dollars, and costing quite a little trouble. Mr. Beecher remarked at the time (during the early eighties) that his lecture was what now seemed to him like "ripping and roaring."

2. *Star Papers, or Experiences of Art and Nature,* 1855. Reappeared 1873 with additional articles selected from more recent writings. These papers contain the glow of the enthusiasm of his first trip to Europe, articles on Ride to Kenilworth, Stratford, Shottery, Oxford, Luxembourg, National Gallery, etc., also his vacation experiences in America.

3. *Life Thoughts,* 1858. Compiled by Edna Dean Proctor. These were gathered from notes taken from the Sabbath sermons and Wednesday evening lectures. "Leaves" which happened to fall into the hands of one or two persons from a "full-boughed tree" "during two successive seasons." — Preface.

4. *Views and Experiences on Religious Subjects*, or New Star Papers, 1859. "These articles were taken for the most part from The New York Independent. If unworthy of a book form the public has itself to blame, in part, for encouraging a like collection of Star Papers some years ago." — H. W. B. They are heart talks, including a famous sermon at Burton's Old Theater on "How to Become a Christian," quoted in full by Dr. Abbott in his first book on Mr. Beecher, prepared with the help of Mr. Halliaday.

5. *Eyes and Ears*, 1862. About one hundred wide-awake articles which appeared first in The New York Ledger under the title, "Thoughts as They Occur to One Who Keeps His Eyes and Ears Open." They are written in happy moods, and "inspire a love for nature." It is the most miscellaneous in the topics of its chapters of all his works. It is written in an easy, offhand style, breezy and wholesome, unstudied, unpretentious, and very characteristic.

6. *Norwood*, 1867. Mr. Beecher's only attempt at fiction, being an interesting tale of New England life, written as a serial for The New York Ledger at the request of Robert Bonner.

7. *Pleasant Talks about Fruits, Flowers and Farming*. Mr. Beecher prepared for these talks by reading Loudon's ponderous tomes, as a let-down from excitement of public speech at Indianapolis. They are very dry reading for most people, but the "talks" are anything but dry.

8. *Prayers*. Several volumes. (*a*) Prayers from Plymouth Pulpit. A. C. Armstrong and Son, 1895. (*b*) Prayers in the Congregation, selected by Rev. J. R. Brown. James Clarke and Company, London, 1886. (*c*) A Book of Prayer. Fords, Howard and Hulbert, 1892. (*d*) Aids to Prayer. Beecher, Anson D. F. Randolph and Company, New York. (No date.)

9. *Beecher as a Humorist*, Eleanor Kirk. Fords,

Howard and Hulbert, 1887. Extracts from his public
utterances. Mr. Beecher owed much to the spontaneity
of humor, and this is the only volume set apart for this
phase of his power.

10. *Lecture Room Talks*, 1870. Pages 378. I. B. Ford
and Company. The very best book by which to get close

A little known picture of Mr. Beecher

to Mr. Beecher as he appeared at the week-night prayer
meetings of Plymouth Church. This contains his parting
words on the occasion of his second trip to Europe in 1863.

11. *A Summer Parish*, 1875. I. B. Ford and Company. Sermons at the Twin Mountain House, New Hamp-
shire. 1874. Very interesting, but out of print.

12. *Religion and Duty.* James Clarke and Company,
London, 1887. "Sunday" readings from Henry Ward

Beecher, selected and arranged by Rev. J. Reeves Brown.
We have here, not the ordinary short selections, but fifty-two
chapters.

13. *Royal Truths*, "reported from the spoken words
of Mr. Beecher." This has passed through very many
editions, from 1866 to 1887. An anthology.

14. Henry Ward Beecher's Last Sermons, preached in
Plymouth Church, Brooklyn, after his return from England,
October, 1886. London, James Clarke and Company, 1887.

INCIDENTS AND
PERSONAL MEMORIES
OF BEECHER

MR. BEECHER IN PRIVATE LIFE

By Rossiter W. Raymond

MR. BEECHER's private life was at all times domi-
nated by a consciousness of his public functions as a
minister, and especially his work as a preacher, with
which he allowed nothing to interfere. Diet, rest,
study, recreation, conversation — all were regulated
with reference to this. He gave up attending the
Philharmonic concerts, then given on Saturday nights,
because his keen enjoyment of them excited and
exhausted him, whereas his rule was to rest before
his work rather than afterwards. For the same reason
he avoided hearty meals, and would not even talk
much, if he could avoid it, on Saturday nights or other
occasions immediately preceding the discharge of his
duty in the pulpit.

As I have elsewhere more fully explained, Mr.
Beecher's mental life had three characteristic and
recurrent phases. First, and longest enduring, was
his habitual actively inquiring and receptive mood, in
which he accumulated facts, hints, impressions and
conclusions as intellectual food. In this mood he
studied, watched, talked and pondered. It was the
atmosphere in which his sermons grew until they
were ripe, from the seeds planted in his little pocket
note-book or in separate compartments of his memory.

Then came his creative mood, in which his faculties were intensely and harmoniously cooperative, so

that he could flash forth, in a complete, comprehensive, pictorial whole, the result of the long accumulation of materials and of many meditations thereon. This rarely lasted more than one or two hours, and was followed by the third phase, a reaction, in which reason and memory seemed to be resting in sleep while the mind recovered its normal tone and strength.*

* After this long lapse of time I may, without impropriety, relate the following incident, hitherto untold. During the first public excitement over the slanderous personal charges brought against Mr. Beecher, and the investigation of them by a committee of Plymouth Church, it was, of course, necessary that he should prepare a complete statement of facts. For this he had to rely upon memory. His adversaries had carefully preserved all documents; he had none.

To facilitate his preparation of this statement a stenographer was employed to take his oral narrative, for his subsequent correction and approval. But we found that, after talking for an hour or two to the stenographer, he could go no further that day. To the question, "What happened next?" he would say only, "I don't remember." And at the following session it would sometimes be difficult to revive the train of thought or recollection thus suspended.

This was annoying enough, in view of the continual public clamor for Mr. Beecher's personal statement and the use made by his accusers of every day's delay. But the statement was at last finished and published; and nothing which it contained was ever successfully impugned, for his memory, when active, was as accurate as a photograph. But the eminent lawyers who represented him in the subsequent lawsuit were overwhelmed with anxiety, amounting to consternation, by the thought that, upon the witness stand, their client might exhibit such relapses in mental activity. "Good heavens!" said one of them, "what if Mr. Beecher, under cross-examination, should begin to say, 'I don't remember?'"

I think this was the most serious fear attending the conduct of his case, in which, as a young layman, I assisted the legal counsel and was admitted to their private consultations. Mr. Beecher alone seemed to be free from anxiety. He felt sure of divine protection; and the rest of us could only pray that such protection might be manifested in the particular way which seemed best to *us* — which is, I fancy, the fashion of most of our prayers! At all events, our gratitude and joy may easily be imagined when Mr. Beecher went through several days of direct and cross-examination without a single lapse of memory, proving himself at all points superior to the art of the eminent lawyer who had been specially engaged to cross-examine him, and maintaining intact his simple, truthful story. To us, who knew the critical nature of this test and the mental habits which handicapped him, this seemed indeed a "special" providence. *He* took it as an ordinary one.

Probably all intellectual workers know these three phases, but I have never met another man who so thoroughly understood, obeyed and managed them. Those of us who are not bound to be "in the Spirit" at a given hour on a given day, may wait idly until the Spirit moves us. But Mr. Beecher took care to make himself ready for the needed inspiration, and to receive it into a brain refreshed, informed and alert.

It was very frequently in his mood of reaction that he came into the homes of such old friends as could understand and respect it, and therefore it was seldom that he became in such circles the brilliant center of conversation. Many exceptions there were — notable ones — when, roused by some question, he would pour out upon two or three entranced listeners rhapsodies of eloquence or thunders of argument almost surpassing, as it seemed, his public utterances. Sometimes, after such an outburst, he would suddenly depart, saying with affected indignation, "There, now you've got a good sermon that was getting ready to come, and it won't come again!" (In more than one instance it never *did* come again; the powder had been burned.)

On the other hand, I have known him to enter my house without a word, pass through to the library, seat himself there alone, take from his pocket a handful of unset precious stones,* spread them on a sheet of white paper before him, study them, arranging and rearranging them on the paper, and, after half an hour, gather them up and depart as silently as he had come.

* Amethysts, topazes, opals, etc. (not diamonds; he did not love diamonds, and thought the "white stone" of the Apocalypse was an opal), many of them his own, but more of them lent him by friendly lapidaries.

But ordinarily he was not as tired as that. He would be ready for light, cheerful gossip about family matters, and, above all, for the children and their play, in which he loved to share, letting them climb upon his knees or ride upon his back. If strangers were present, before whom he might be expected to "show off," he was very likely to excuse himself after a short call. But if there was nobody to spoil the game there was no telling how long it might last. I remember one evening when Mr. Beecher was telling stories to children and grown folks alike, and bedtime came for the smallest little boy. Climbing reluctantly up the stairs the child turned and shouted down into the parlor, "O, Mr. Beecher, *please* don't say anything after I am gone!" "Not one word!" was the reply; and Mr. Beecher immediately arose and (after the usual hunt for his hat) bade us all good-night, and went out, slamming the front door, so that his little friend might know he had kept his promise!

Curiously enough, Mr. Beecher, so bold in any public or representative capacity, was, in private, shy and bashful. In moments of strong personal feeling he took refuge in silence. He told me once (when he was past sixty) that he never entered without embarrassment a room in which he expected to find strangers. "But," he added, "on the platform I am another man. *There* I am not afraid of anything or anybody. I have a consciousness of command. If there should be an alarm of fire I *know* that I could make the crowd obey me and sit still, or go out quietly." (He was right as to that; I have seen him do it.)

Dr. Lyman Abbott, in his recent admirable book on Mr. Beecher, speaks of him as going rapidly through books and getting the heart out of them. But that was only his way of testing books before deciding whether to read them. For he was a slow reader, even of light literature. Books on science, philosophy, history, etc., he read and reread, often turning back to passages which had been to him, upon first perusal, impressive or suggestive. In such books (lent to me after he had read them) I often found heavy marginal pencil marks, evidently intended simply to help him in finding certain paragraphs again. I do not remember (with one exception) any which implied approval or disapproval. Knowing his mental attitude and method in particular lines of study, I have recognized, among the passages thus marked, some which he doubted, some which admirably stated his own views, and some which he doubtless deemed fundamentally wrong and logically weak. But most of the marked paragraphs were simply points in the author's argument. For it was characteristic of him that he read such a book to get the author's standpoint, method and message.

In one instance within my knowledge (of course there may have been others) Mr. Beecher wrote in a volume his opinion of it. It was "Lorna Doone," which he had borrowed of me, and on the title-page of which I found, when he returned it, these penciled words :

This book is like a capital fowl, somewhat overstuffed, and a trifle too long in the oven ; otherwise, a dish fit for a king.   H. W. B.

But it should be noted that Mr. Beecher read different books for different purposes. Some simply instructed him; some stimulated him, suggesting more than they said; some refreshed and soothed him; some could put him to sleep. And he kept examples of each sort always at hand, to be used according to his mood or need.

One day, finding him absorbed in a "gorgeous" novel by Ouida, I expressed my surprise that, being so slow a reader, he should waste time upon such a story. His reply was, "She has a wonderful vocabulary, and I am reading for *that*." It was the oratorical element (in itself a blemish) in Ouida's style that attracted him.

His own writing was as impulsive, fluent and abundant as his speech. Accustomed for so many years to throw off hasty "copy" for the printer, and to write out or leave unwritten, as the mood seized him, passages in his sermons, he had come, apparently, to regard the pen as a simple alternative of the tongue; and he wrote letters, sometimes without date, sometimes without signature, sometimes without address, sometimes forgetting to finish them or mail them, and always, I think, without retaining copies of them.

The following hitherto unpublished letter may serve as an illustration. It was found, after Mr. Beecher's death, among his papers. Nobody knows to whom it was addressed, or whether it was ever sent.

BROOKLYN, May 8th, 1867.

Dear Sir: I do not think Science, *as it will be*, is without its Calvary. But, *as it now is*, in the hands of Mill,

Spencer, Huxley, Tyndall and, I may add, Charles Darwin, it has gone only so far as to have lost the cross, and not far enough to have found it again.

I am entirely confident that the truths of the New Testament are perfectly at one with the truth of nature. Both are divine. They will never collide in any such sense as to be interchangeably destructive.

We are in a transition. Such periods are apt to be barrens and deserts for religious feeling. I am anxious to maintain the religious sentiment and fervor of men during these changes, and that recasting of philosophy which impends.   Yours truly,

HENRY WARD BEECHER.

If this letter was never sent, it may be that Mr. Beecher was not entirely satisfied with its phraseology. But from my knowledge of him I am inclined to think that he meant, and simply forgot, to mail it. At all events, it expresses substantially his own solemn personal injunction to me, which I here publicly repeat, I think for the first time (though I have repeated it in conversation heretofore) :

When I am gone, do not let it be forgotten that my one aim was the winning of the souls of men for Jesus Christ; that I have restated old doctrines in new language for this purpose — to make them acceptable to living men — and not out of desire for destruction or innovation. My business has always been, and will always be, not to make theology, but to save men by bringing them to Christ.

This was his habitual consciousness and attitude. He was a congenial associate in all sorts of company ; but he never "let himself down," morally, for any company ; and all who met him, however informally, were made to feel that behind and above his cordial fellowship there was an ever-present sacred mission and purpose. This, at least, was my experience. I knew Mr. Beecher as intimately as most, and in some respects more intimately than any of his friends outside of his own family; and I bear witness that no degree of familiarity ever impaired the affectionate reverence with which I regarded him.

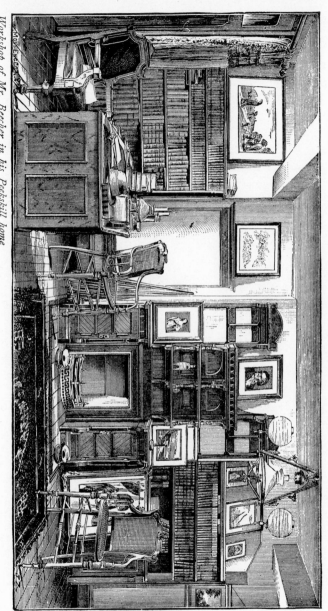

Workshop of Mr. Beecher in his Peekskill home

THE HENRY WARD BEECHER OF MY CHILDHOOD

By Rev. R. DeW. Mallary, Housatonic, Mass.

As I look back upon my boyhood days in Plymouth Church, Brooklyn, the first picture to come before me is the Sunday morning congregation. Pewholders had to be in their seats ten minutes before the opening of service, and we used to make our way to our pew through ranks of waiting strangers. And what a vast, expectant assemblage it was when John Zundel started in on the voluntary; a congregation never quite the same, perhaps twenty-five per cent. being "strangers within the gates." Pulpit stairs, aisles, second gallery, all chock-full and crowds standing about the doors.

The central figure in it all, Mr. Beecher, seemed perfectly self-possessed, and surveyed the assemblage with a quiet dignity. He had no assistant minister then to take the devotional part of the worship, and in this part he was, indeed, unique. Unconventional, he possessed a beautiful sense of pulpit proprieties. He caught the ear of all at the start by low tones, almost inaudible. How deliberately, reverently, impressively he read the Scripture! And how fond he was of reading the thirteenth chapter of First Corinthians! How comprehensively, unctuously, directly he prayed!—his prayers were litanies, communions. And such singing from that immense congregation! Will I ever hear its like again?

In sermon-time, often lasting over an hour, my
attention flagged or wandered. I fear I counted the
bald heads in a given row of seats, and noted the
rapidly-flying stenographer's pencil, but all the same
I heard a good deal. Mr. Beecher's sermons were
canvases; he preached in pictures, and I often was a
rapt little hearer. The congregation now clapped and
then cried, swayed absolutely by the great mind and
soul that throbbed aloud a message of truth and love
and duty!

I have many detached memories of Mr. Beecher
and Plymouth Church during those early days. Mr.
Beecher's illustrious father sometimes moved up and
down our Sunday-school aisles, stopping here and
there for a kindly word. There were no Sunday
horse-cars in Brooklyn then, and Mr. Beecher advocated this "new departure," bringing to an end a
Sabbatic quiet that had hitherto reigned on the first
day of the week and incidentally covering himself
with an avalanche of criticism. His leading opponent
in this matter thereafter, it was said, patronized the
livery stables when he had occasion to travel on the
Sabbath. War memories, too, group themselves about
those early days. I was too young to comprehend all
I saw and heard, but my father, who was a stanch
Democrat, came home from church one day in high
dudgeon. Mr. Beecher had had that morning in the
service a slave in the pulpit with him, and had kissed
her before the entire congregation. That was too
much for my father, and for a year he went alone to
the Congregational church across the street, where
William Alvin Bartlett was then trying his pulpit

powers.   Needless to say he came back, and was to
the last day of his long life one of Mr. Beecher's
warmest admirers and defenders.   During the mobs
in New York a missile came whizzing through a pane
of glass one evening while Plymouth Church was at
service, and we read the next morning of the cordon
of police that escorted Mr. Beecher home that night,
while the mob wreaked its vengeance on the "abolitionist" by painting his brownstone front with lamp-
black.   We boys went down a few days after to see
the almost indelible smut which remained there for
many a year.

I cannot speak at any length of other "events"
which made an impression on my boy mind : the New
Years' receptions at Mr. Beecher's house to which
my father always took me; the return of Mr. Beecher
from Europe and Palestine in 1863, and the disappear-
ance of an old rampart sort of a pulpit to make way
for the simple furniture made of olive-wood selected
by Mr. Beecher in the Holy Land; the deeply impressive baptismal services when Mr. Beecher used to
immerse those candidates preferring that method of
administering the rite.

I cannot remember that Mr. Beecher often came
into our Sunday-school.   He certainly had no class.
Yet it would be a mistake to suppose he took no interest in this part of the church work.   His hand was
felt in all the departments of the parish life.   All the
world knows his fondness for flowers, birds and nature.
Our Sunday-school had a fountain in the center of the
room.   One end of my quadrant-shaped bench abutted
on the aisle next to that musical *jet d'eau*, and I used

to watch, between the questions, the gold and silver fish swimming around among the moss-covered rocks. Around three sides of the room were galleries for primary scholars, Bible classes and "visitors." The visitors' gallery was always filled. Underneath these galleries were hanging flower baskets and bird-cages, so that Sunday was the best day of the week and Sunday-school the eager anticipation of my weekdays.

Mr. Beecher came to our sessions seldom, but when he came he was in his happiest mood, and certainly his was the moving spirit behind those happy Sunday-school hours. They are among the most precious of childhood's memories. They taught me by the inspirations they gave me — sometimes oppressive inspirations — to have confidence in the susceptibility of every boy's and girl's soul to God.

Only a few more days and we shall be on our way to Peekskill where I will roll on the grass, frolic with the dogs, rejoice in the flowers, sit under the big pine tree and superintend laying out the road, and we will all have a good time generally. But having had it I shall return to my church, ready, happy and eager to resume my labors, and with a heart all the richer in love for it and my people, for these few weeks of rest. — *From a letter of Mr. Beecher's.*

THE UNDERGRADUATE DAYS OF
HENRY WARD BEECHER

By Walter A. Dyer

THE story of the college days of Henry Ward
Beecher and the tale of his wooing and his winning are
one. It was during his life at Amherst College, with
its many interests and its vast influences on his subsequent career, that he met, wooed and won the woman
who was to be his companion through all the remarkable events of his after life.

To Amherst, the Village Beautiful, redolent with
Indian traditions and tales of colonial strife, came
Henry Ward Beecher, three-quarters of a century ago,
in search of learning. He was at that time boyish-
looking and a trifle diffident, with that awkwardness
which comes with rapid growth. Honest eyes and a
frank, open face, now serious, now all mirth, bespoke
a great soul which even then stirred within him, and
which never lost its youthful freshness. Breathing
in the scholarly atmosphere of the old institution with
the sweet, wholesome air of the Hadley meadows and
the Pelham hills, Beecher grew from boyhood to manhood. Years afterward he said, "I owe more to what
God has done for Amherst than anything he ever did
for me."

Beecher fitted at the Mt. Pleasant Classical Insti-
tute in Amherst, and entered college in 1830. There
were forty students in his class. The college was

then but nine years old, small and poorly endowed, but the chairs of instruction were filled by scholars and men of strong personality. Rev. Dr. Heman Humphrey, a renowned theologian, was president.

Beecher's academic career at Amherst was a peculiar one, and his attitude toward the prescribed course of study has given rise to some controversy. There is a tradition current among the undergraduates which certain professors, and among them the late Prof. W. S. Tyler, in his "History of Amherst College," have in vain endeavored to explain away, that throughout his course Beecher stood at the foot of his class. As direct evidence on this point, Rev. S. Hopkins Emery, of Taunton, Massachusetts, one of Beecher's classmates at Amherst College, said, in a letter to the present chronicler:

Beecher, I am sorry to say, paid little attention to the prescribed course of study in college, so that he might about as well have been elsewhere so far as study in the regular course was concerned. I think he regretted it afterward. Of course he had brain enough to have easily led the class, if his ambition and taste had so dictated; but the fact that he was one of the few who failed of any Commencement appointment proves what I have said about it. Of course he was not idle. He thought and read much.

Beecher himself said that he stood next the head of his class only once in his course, on a day when the class was arranged in a circle.

Beecher was, however, the leading debater in college, and his devotion to this exercise proved invaluable training for his life-work. It was in the preparation for one of his debates on the question of African colonization that the conviction of the human rights of

the Southern slaves first came to him.   Lewis Tappan,
a classmate, said of him : " In logic and class debates
no one could approach him.   I listened to his flow of
impassioned eloquence in those my youthful days with
wonder and admiration."   Rev. Mr. Emery remembered that Henry Clay visited Amherst once during
those days, and some of the students presented him
with a Bible.   Beecher made the presentation speech,
for no one else was considered so well fitted to do
it, and the smooth-faced young fellow won the great
statesman's praise.

Beecher's written essays also attracted considerable attention, chiefly because of their originality of
thought; but his chief study was nature and her
moods, and frequently in his sermons afterward he
referred to incidents which occurred and impressions
which he received while on long, solitary tramps
among the hills and woods which lie about the
beautiful New England town.   Still, he was always
appreciative of the advantages of his college.   He
once said, long afterward, in public reference to those
days of endeavor, that he owed his inspiration for
manly living to three persons — his dead mother,
whose spirit seemed ever near him as a guardian
angel; a negro servant who chopped wood and sang
hymns in his father's shed; and the professor of
mathematics in Amherst College.

Beecher at one time took up the study of phrenology, and, in company with a classmate, Orson S.
Fowler, went about among the neighboring towns
lecturing.   This interest, however, soon gave place to
that in the cause of temperance, for which he became
an active worker and an eloquent lecturer.

He was a contributor to The Shrine, the undergraduate publication, was a prominent member of
the Athenian debating society, and was interested in
several departments of college activity. Soon after
his graduation, in 1837, he became one of the honor-
ary charter members of the Amherst chapter of the
Alpha Delta Phi fraternity.

Beecher's love of fun was irresistible, and the few
anecdotes which are told of him are characteristic.
They are most of them too well known to need
repetition here. His poverty, his queer room, with
its round table, and other circumstances of his college
life have often been recounted. At one time he became the champion of his class in an interclass dis-
pute, and so won the enmity of a Junior who afterwards became a famous lawyer and voluntarily took
active part in the case against Beecher at the time
of the scandal in Plymouth Church, Brooklyn, and
well-nigh had his revenge.

And so the days flitted by in beautiful Amherst.
A letter written by Beecher to his sister during his
Junior year, which is one of the few of this period
which have been preserved, is to be found among the
memorabilia in the college library at Amherst. It
gives an insight into many of his thoughts and sentiments. He was a young man of moods, and highly
susceptible to religious excitement and depression.
At one time the reaction from a religious revival in
the college threw him into a period of spiritual gloom.
He found plenty of precept, but not the sympathy
which he sought. He was left for a long time to fight
it out almost alone, with but one companion who was

able to understand, one Moody Harrington, whom he
remembered long afterward with affectionate gratitude.
Then came the love of a good woman, and the skies
cleared.

Beecher's most intimate friend in college was
E. W. Bullard, who roomed with him for several
terms. He was the son of Rev. Artemus Bullard,
and his home was in West Sutton, Massachusetts.[1]
He had two brothers who were afterwards eminent
in their profession : Rev. Artemus Bullard, Jr., long
a leading Presbyterian clergyman in St. Louis, who
met a sad death in a dreadful railroad disaster near
that city ; and Rev. Asa Bullard, in his day one of
the best-known Congregational ministers in New England. Young Bullard and Henry Beecher formed
one of those close college friendships which never
wear out.

The two were just out of their Freshman year
when, together with another classmate, they walked
from Amherst to West Sutton, fifty miles, to spend
their spring vacation at Dr. Bullard's. Mrs. Bullard
was on the porch to greet them, and with her was her
daughter Eunice, a pretty, red-cheeked country girl,
affectionate and modest. As she stood there, with
the afternoon sun gilding her hair, she presented a
picture which remained in Beecher's heart for many
a day.

He was lonely and troubled, and nothing could
have been more welcome than that quiet New England home and the sympathy of a gentle maiden.
Beecher was only a boy, and Eunice, though ten
months his senior, was an unsophisticated country

girl. Yet they talked of grave matters, and Beecher did his best to appear favorably in her eyes. When, one evening, he made a slip, it worried him out of all proportion to the fault. They were talking, the three classmates, about a friend whose recent engagement they did not approve.

"She can't sing a note," said Beecher, "and who would want a girl that couldn't sing?"

Later in the evening some one asked Eunice to sing and she declined, saying that it was not one of her accomplishments. That night Henry Ward Beecher went to bed very unhappy.

But the days drifted quickly by, and Beecher went back to college with a newer purpose and a lighter heart. And when at last he spoke of love it was all very quaint and very awkward, but beautiful in its sincerity. During the summer and fall after their first meeting Eunice taught school in Clappville, Massachusetts. Henry secured a position in North-bridge soon afterward, and was able to see her sometimes. During his winter vacation he went to live with her aunt in Whiting's Village, where she was staying, ostensibly to help her in Latin, though she knew more of the classics than he.

Then Eunice said, quietly, "Why, I can't sing, and only a short time since you said you would never marry a woman who could not sing."

Henry laughed.

"Oh, that was six months ago, and I have changed my mind."

"And in six months more you may change it again," said she.

"No, I changed it the minute you said you never sang," he answered. "There is no fear of my changing it again."

And her heart told her that he spoke true.

That was January 2, 1832. Henry was not a youth to delay matters. The next Saturday he went to West Sutton and told Dr. and Mrs. Bullard what had happened. The father was angry and the mother grieved.

"Why, you are a couple of babes," said Dr. Bullard, and Henry could only blush and stammer. But at last the parents were won over by his earnest appeal.

The course of love ran not wholly smooth, even then. Beecher had no money, and he longed to show his young *fiancée* some material token of his love. He worked hard teaching school at West Sutton and delivering temperance lectures. For one of these he received five dollars. With this he purchased a copy of Baxter's "Saints' Rest" for Eunice — a gift somewhat uncommon in these days of violets and bonbons. During one vacation he walked all the way to Brattleboro, Vermont, where he received the enormous sum of ten dollars for a lecture. A ring was bought with this, which served both as an engagement and a wedding gift.

Life had now a new meaning for Beecher, and when he became one of the great names in American history he loved to look back to those early, hard, sweet days when he was an undergraduate at Amherst — and in love.

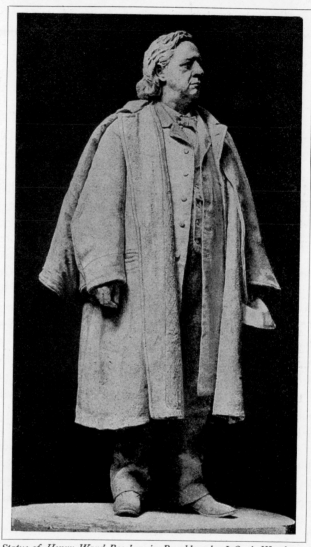

Statue of Henry Ward Beecher, in Brooklyn, by J. Q. A. Ward

MR. BEECHER AND THE TWO PLYMOUTH BOYS

By Edward Bok

It is a popular impression that Henry Ward Beecher had little idea of the value of money — that he let it slip through his fingers. This was true, in a sense. And yet I remember an instance that will, perhaps, illustrate that money did have a meaning to him under certain conditions.

A friend of mine and I had induced Mr. Beecher to write a weekly article dealing with current events, which we were to publish simultaneously in a number of newspapers — a "syndicate," in other words. He was very skeptical of the result. "No one has ever yet succeeded in making money out of my supposed literary work," he said, "and you won't." But we persisted. We had all the confidence of youth. We agreed to pay Mr. Beecher a sum of three figures per week. We were two of his boys —-his "Plymouth boys" — and, of course, he knew that the amount we agreed to pay him was considerable — for us.

When the first article had been written we brought him our first check. He looked at it quizzically and then at us. Finally he said, "Thank you." He took a pin and pinned the check to his desk. There it remained. The following week he wrote another article, and we gave him another check. He pinned that up over the other.

"I like to look at them, you know," was his only explanation as he saw my look of curiosity.

The third check was treated in the same way, and when we handed him the fourth one morning, and he was pinning it up over the others, he asked,

"When do you get your money from the newspapers?"

We told him we were sending out bills that morning for the four letters constituting a month's service.

A fortnight passed, and one day Mr. Beecher asked,

"Well, how are the checks coming in?"

"Very well," we assured him.

"Suppose you let me see how much you've got in," he suggested one morning, and we brought the accounts to him.

"You do not get quite so much out of it as I do," was his comment. We told him we didn't expect to; that it would pay us well if we got half as much, and that we would get more as the service grew.

"That's very interesting," he said. "How much have you in the bank?"

We told him our balance less the checks we gave to him.

"But I haven't turned them in yet," he explained. "Anyhow, you have gotten in enough to meet the checks you have given me and a profit besides, haven't you?"

We assured him we had.

Then taking his bank-book from a drawer, he took down the six checks pinned on his desk, wrote a deposit slip, and handing the book to me said,

"Just hand that in at the bank as you go by, will you?"

I was very young then, and Mr. Beecher's methods of financiering seemed to me quite in line with current notions of his lack of business knowledge. But as the years rolled on the incident took on a new phase — such a strong, magnificent phase!

It seemed so inexplicable then; it is so beautifully considerate now. I did not thank him then; I wish I could now.

THE BEECHER RIFLES CHURCH

By C. M. Harger, Abilene, Kansas

Out on the Kansas prairie, at Wabaunsee, not many miles from the geological center of the United States, stands a stone church that is a memorial to the patriotism of one of the world's greatest preachers, Henry Ward Beecher, and his congregation, and to a devotion to the cause of freedom that makes the place twice hallowed. It is also a monument to the bravery of Christian pioneers in a sense possessed by no other structure in the West.

Each spring the people of the little prairie community celebrate the anniversary of the building of the church, and with singing, prayer and addresses recall the story of its beginning, a story as romantic as many famous in history. It has an inspiration, too, for the believer, in that it tells of the triumph of a strong, brave faith and the upbuilding of a sturdy, patriotic Christianity.

A Letter of Mr. Beecher's

My dear Children:

I have received from you, through Mr. & Mrs. Fowle, the present of a beautiful suspension vase. and I heartily thank you for it. I am glad that you had such a nice Christmas. & such a beautiful tree, & so many presents, & that you enjoyed yourselves so much—

I have placed the
swinging Vase on my
mantlepiece, and
shall keep it for
flowers. And every time
I see the buds blossom
I shall think of the
dear little Children
that so kindly remember
him. Yours affectionately

Henry Ward Beecher

Brooklyn Dec 30. 1871.

In 1856, when the interest in the Nebraska-Kansas Bill was at its height and the New England States were more than usually awake to the importance of the new territory being a free state, a meeting was held at New Haven to enroll men to go to the new country to live and to fight.   Henry Ward Beecher made a stirring address. At the close it was announced that one hundred men had joined the party, but that, while they were well prepared to dig and plow, they were not in shape to fight.

Professor Silliman, of Yale College, rose and subscribed twenty-five dollars to buy one rifle, and urged that the colonists be fully armed before they set out.

A thrilling scene followed.   Beecher, then at the zenith of his power and with all the eloquence of his best days, took the rostrum and promised to see that half the rifles were furnished from his own congregation.   He blessed the new plans and bade the men Godspeed.   In a few days he sent guns for every man, over six hundred dollars having been subscribed by his church for the purpose.   Along with the guns were a Bible and a hymn-book for each colonist.

On the last day of March they took their way toward the setting sun, going down the streets of New Haven watched by thousands.   It was as fine a body of men as ever started for the new lands — doctors, lawyers, merchants, teachers and preachers — and every one carried on his shoulder a rifle, in his pocket a hymn-book and a Bible, and in his heart a firm determination to wield a power for freedom in the wilderness, no matter what the cost.

The journey was long and dangerous, but they

took their way across the Mississippi, on into the
prairies and up the valley of the Kaw.

On the way they formed a cooperative organization
and bought shovels, axes and other tools with which
to fit themselves and their families, who were to come
after, with homes.

Each Sabbath the preacher who was chosen as
their pastor read the inspiring words given them with
the rifles by Mr. Beecher when they started West :

Let these arms hang above your doors as the old
Revolutionary muskets do in many New England homes.
May your children in another generation look upon them
with pride and say, "Our fathers' courage saved this fair
land from slavery and blood." Every morning's breeze shall
catch the blessings of our prayers and roll them westward
to your prairie homes. May your sons be large-hearted as
the heavens above your heads; may your daughters fill the
land as the flowers do the prairies, only sweeter and fairer
than they. You will not need to use arms when it is known
that you have them. It is the essence of slavery to be
arrogant before the weak and cowardly before the strong.

These words are also read at the annual meetings
in commemoration of the coming of the brave pioneers
to the plains.

The Beecher Rifles colony, as it was called, had
able men in it. More than a score of Yale College
diplomas went along with the rifles and Bibles. Rev.
Harvey Brown, the first pastor, held meetings in a
grove and later in a tent. Once there was an alarm
of Indians during a service. Hastily the hymn-books
were exchanged for rifles, and away the congregation
went to defend the homes and families. The raid was
stopped and the colony saved. Then there was a
meeting of thankfulness.

In 1862 they built the church that yet stands a
monument to the devotion of the early days.   It is
rude in architecture and plain in all its belongings.
But it is the incarnation of the pioneer spirit, and in
it are still held meetings where attend many of the
original pioneers, now getting well along the pathway
of life.   Rev. F. D. Jackson is the present pastor.

Beecher Rifles Church, Wabaunsee, Kan.

The fate of the colony was of constant interest to
Beecher, and he sent many messages to the toilers
on the prairie.   The spirit that animated the colonists
spread over New England, and the emigrant aid soci-
eties and the colonies that took their westward way
were to some extent followers of this movement.   The
anti-slavery movement was typified by the bravery of
this company, and the high character of the colonists

that led in the struggle of the West for freedom was shown by the men who went into the peril of the long journey bearing rifles and Bibles.

The West has many such examples of religious earnestness that won honor and position when the need of the new lands was great. It was because of such sentiments then that there is now so firm a foundation for the schools and churches of the plains. It was a right beginning, and, while there was often a possibility of avoiding use of the rifles, the fact that vigor could be used if needed made the respect for the colonists the greater.

The little stone church standing out on the prairies teaches a lesson of faith and courage. Of such material as its builders was the foundation of freedom laid.

MR. BEECHER'S YALE LECTURES

By Prof. George P. Fisher

Mr. Beecher lectured on "Preaching" in the Divinity School at Yale for three consecutive years, on the foundation established by his parishioner and close friend, Mr. Henry W. Sage. No doubt it was Mr. Sage's admiration of Mr. Beecher's gifts as a preacher, and wish that young men looking forward to the ministry might acquaint themselves with his characteristic methods and peculiar charm, that led to the endowment of the Lyman Beecher Lectureship. The prolonged task was fulfilled by Mr. Beecher with not the smallest sign of weariness on his part, or the least waning of interest on the part of the audiences that flocked to the Marquand Chapel to listen to him. He spoke with no other written aid than brief notes jotted on pieces of paper hardly larger than the palm of his hand. All who heard him — the younger theologues and the older professors and pastors — felt that the speaker combined in himself, with the talents, seldom surpassed, of an orator, the genius of a poet — albeit he did not compose verses — and of a humorist, and was a speaker whom it cost no effort to move his auditors to tears or to laughter.

Mr. Beecher's lectures, not being written, were taken down shorthand in the delivery of them, and owing to the pressure of his occupations they were given to the press without revision. Notwithstanding this disadvantage, they are, as printed, characterized by lucid arrangement of the contents, and they are marked by luminous statement and careful discrimination. He told the young men that the ideal of a true Christian preacher is "to take the great truths of the Lord Jesus Christ's teachings, and the love of God to the human race, and make them a part of his own personal experience, so that when he speaks to men it shall not be he alone that speaks, but God in him." Fitly mated with this saying is the most excellent opening discourse of Phillips Brooks in *his* Yale lectures. Mr. Beecher pointed out to the theological pupils before him another prime necessity in their calling : "A part of your preparation for the Christian ministry consists in such a ripening of your disposition that you yourselves shall be exemplars of what you preach." They must *live by faith* — "the sense of the infinite and the invisible." He declared that

power to be of priceless value which he said that he
had derived by inheritance from his mother — the
power "to see the unseeable," "to realize things"
not present to the senses.

This reference to his mother brings to mind the
habit of Mr. Beecher to interweave not so very in-
frequently, in lectures and sermons, allusions to his
kinsfolk — incidents relating to his father, to a brother,
or some other near kinsman.   These anecdotes sometimes bordered on the jocose, and might pass the
limits of a reserve as to domestic concerns which is
generally considered becoming.   There was a deep
well of tenderness and pathos in the great preacher's
heart.   But this precious endowment is not always
coincident with faultless refinement.   Of this fact
there are numerous examples ; Martin Luther is one
signal instance.   The oratory of Mr. Beecher, with
its fulness of energy and warmth, was thought by not
over-fastidious critics to touch at times the fringe, at
least, of vulgarity.   Matthew Arnold, who at least
learned to estimate his merit justly, was tempted to
style him "a heated barbarian."   He was led in his
ardor, at times, to intermingle with his oratory the
extraneous leaven of mimicry, failing thus to keep
apart the provinces of the orator and the actor.

Mr. Beecher in his Yale lectures gave sufficient
evidence of that ability to distinguish between things
that differ, and to deal with the distinctions and
problems of philosophy, which proved that he was
no stranger to culture in the region of abstract
thought.   He showed a facility in putting to a homi-
letic use his acquisitions there.   His exaggerated

valuation of phrenology carried with it the custom
of availing himself of its not inconvenient classifica-
tion of mental qualities and functions. Undeniably
it would have been a source of increased power had
Mr. Beecher, with the actual development of his native
faculties, his fertility in thought and imagination, and
the knowledge that he gathered from varied sources,
blended a more complete and rigorous discipline during the years of study and preparation for his career —
very brilliant and successful in many directions though
it was.

Certainly in the pretty long list of the lecturers on
the Lyman Beecher foundation, comprising so many
eminent names, American and foreign, none — not
even Brooks, or Dale, or Taylor — were heard with
more eagerness, none whose teachings gave more
satisfaction when they were uttered, or have been
longer retained in memory. The robust figure of the
captivating orator, as he stood on the platform at
the side of the desk and poured out of a heart and
mind overflowing with thought and feeling — all seem-
ing to be the inspiration of the moment — a stream
of wisdom and wit — that image, one may be sure,
never perished from the recollections of the successive
generations of students who prized so highly the privilege of hearing him and of proposing to him on the
spot questions to be instantly answered in pertinent
replies, seasoned with pleasantry.

A YOUNG THEOLOGUE'S IMPRESSIONS
OF BEECHER

By Rev. Hugh Pedley, Montreal

My first memory of the name of Beecher goes back to my boyhood in Newfoundland, when we caught echoes of the war of the secession and heard men speak in the same breath of Lincoln, Grant and Beecher. My first sight of the great preacher was in 1873, when he gave an address in old Zion Church, Montreal, on the occasion of the opening of the session of the Congregational college. Our little band of students was there in the front pews and he spoke to *us*, unconscious of the rest of the audience. We felt the power of the man's personality and the magnificence of his sorrow, for it was the time when his good name was under menace, as he said:

"Young men, I have seen much of life, I have known men who have achieved success as bankers, statesmen, warriors, actors, but I am here to tell you that had I my life to live over again I would choose no other path than the one along which I have come, that of a minister of the gospel of Jesus Christ."

My next contact was during the Christmas vacation of 1876. Sunday morning found me one of the great and expectant throng of worshipers in Plymouth Church. As the service in Trinity Church, Boston, under the leadership of Phillips Brooks, was the acme of that solemnity, reverence and splendor of which a

115

liturgical worship is capable, so this service in Plymouth Church, conducted by Mr. Beecher, was the highest expression of the dignified freedom, joyousness and direct touch of the human upon the divine which may be found in a worship that dispenses with formal ritual. The prayers were the speech of a child to its father, the plea of a friend for his friends, the supplication of a patriot for his country.

The sermon lasted hardly more than an hour. It was an argument to prove that in human life the joyous element predominates; but the argument, which in the hands of some men would have been bare and hard as a train track in a Pennsylvania colliery, was, under his treatment, a pathway bordered with flowers, glistening with dew, and opening up glimpses of the vastness of the ocean and the sublimity of mountain crests. It was my somewhat unique experience to hear Mr. Beecher make use of a quotation, and this, too, as an introduction to his sermon. This was the quotation:

> Lord, what a wretched land is this
> That yields us no supply,
> No cheering fruits, no wholesome trees
> Nor streams of living joy!

And then the comment. "The man that wrote that didn't deserve to have any." A gentle ripple of smiles passed over the faces of the people, and by the time that had vanished the preacher was fully under way in the great optimistic argument which formed the backbone of his sermon. A day or so before I left Montreal, the pastor of Zion Church had suddenly lost his young wife. As I sat in Plymouth

Church that Sunday morning and shared in the warmth and uplift of the service, the wish suddenly arose in my heart that the stricken man might be within these walls. And whom should I see the next Sunday morning, at the close of the service, but the bereaved young pastor in one of the side seats, and Mr. Beecher with his arm affectionately thrown around him and speaking such words of sympathy as only he could speak.

It was my privilege one Sunday morning to have a few minutes' conversation with Mr. Beecher. I was a theological student full of doubts. What I said I do not remember, but my listener at once took in the situation. "You may have your doubts," he said, "about inspiration, the atonement and future punishment, but there is one thing you cannot doubt, and it is this, that men need building up in spiritual manhood, and the New Testament is of all books the one best fitted for that work." When I said that I envied him his faith, his vivid consciousness of the Unseen, he answered me very quietly and gravely. "That," he said, "is a thing that grows."

AN EVENING HOUR AT HENRY WARD BEECHER'S HOME

By Rev. A. S. Walker, D.D.

WHILE a student at Union Theological Seminary, as often as possible I attended the mid-week lecture at Plymouth Church. It so happened one evening that the topic was one with which I had had considerable difficulty, nor did Mr. Beecher's presentation of it

leave the matter quite clear. This I frankly stated
to him at the close of the service, and in his very
informal and friendly way he took my arm in his and
said — as cordially as if I had been his own younger
brother — "Come home with me and we will talk the
matter over by ourselves."

Of course I availed myself of his friendly offer;
and after a conference in his study the difficulty,
under the illumination of his wonderful mind, seemed
wholly to vanish.   •

His father at that time was living with him; and
after our talk he said, "Now I want you to come into
the parlor and meet my father." I hardly need say
that I required no urging, and I now look back upon
that social hour as one of the brightest spots in my
student life. Both father and son were in their happiest mood, and there passed between them the merriest
banter imaginable.

One of his stories at his father's expense was as
follows. Turning to me he said : "Do you see that
painting on the wall yonder? Well, I had always
thought that my father's one failing was a lack of
appreciation for fine art. His mind was so given
up to preaching and theology that there seemed little
liking for anything else. But when I brought that
painting home it attracted his attention immediately.
He would stand before it a quarter of an hour at a
time. I felt very greatly encouraged. I was so glad
that a taste for the fine arts was really developing,
even though so late in life. One day as he was standing before it I observed that he was talking to himself.
I drew near very quietly, being curious. It seems that

the artist had endeavored to put a little life into the landscape by introducing in one corner a hunter who had just fired into a flock of ducks. And my father was saying to himself, ' Well, that fellow has dropped two of his ducks anyway, and there is that third that won't manage to get far away!' Then," said Henry Ward, " I gave my father up so far as fine art was concerned. I found that his interest in the painting was not at all in the art, but simply in the hunter, the picture reminding him of his own fondness for hunting."

"Well," said the father, turning the joke, " I have always found that a minister who could take good aim with his gun was likely to take all the better aim with his sermon. And I want to say, for the benefit of this young man here, that I have often thought that if Henry would only take a little better aim in some of his sermons and not scatter round quite so much, he would bring down more birds!"

Then turning to me more directly he continued : " And there is another thing that I think I will just speak of for the benefit of this young man. I have noticed that theological students usually get married as soon as they are through with their seminary course. Somehow the people expect it and the students them- selves don't need any special urging. Now it will be well to be a little careful as to whom you shall marry. When I was a young man I made up my mind to two things. First, that I would never marry a woman that wasn't better looking than I. And I didn't, did I, Henry ? And secondly, that I never would marry a woman that was worth any more money than I. For

I remember a couple down in Connecticut who got married and the man was worth two shillings and the woman two and six; and the man used to say that his wife was forever twitting him on that odd sixpence!"

And so with mirthful story and pleasant banter the evening passed, and I left Brooklyn Heights feeling that wealth of genius may be so combined with warmth of heart that even those who stand highest may yet be sympathetic and accessible to the very humblest, and that a true piety and mirth make admirable companions alike in the oldest as in the youngest heart.

AN EX–SLAVE'S IMPRESSIONS OF HENRY WARD BEECHER

By Maggie Porter Cole

One of the Original Fisk Jubilee Singers

I was a child, a freed slave fresh from the South and slavery, one of the eleven students selected from Fisk University to come North and try by our voices to pay off a debt on the institution.

After many and varied experiences we arrived in New York City, with permission from Mr. Beecher to sing at one of his Friday evening meetings.

I had heard of Henry Ward Beecher as a friend of the negro, as a brother of Mrs. Harriet Beecher Stowe, and knew that these two had played a wonderful part in the emancipation of the slave, but in my wildest dreams I had not imagined myself permitted to sit at his feet with others and listen to wonderful words of love and truth. So that when, with my

associates, I was ushered in and seated in Plymouth
Church, I do not remember which moved me most,
the sight of the great, kindly-faced man who sat and
beamed upon us, or the thought that *we who but
yesterday were slaves* were in such a place of worship,
under such conditions, and were to be allowed to sing
some of our Southern songs here before this great
man.   However, Mr. Beecher's call to come upon the
platform and his reception set us at our ease and
reminded me of the charge Mr. White (our leader)
had given us, "to remember that everything hinged
upon the success of that night."

I watched the emotions play upon Mr. Beecher's
face — and there never was a more expressive face —
as he listened to our songs, and I knew the battle
was won.

We sang twenty minutes, and as we were leaving
the platform Mr. Beecher jumped before us with
pocketbook in hand and told those present he wished
they would let their pockets as well as their hearts
be touched.

The victory was ours.   We had won to our cause
the great-hearted Henry Ward Beecher.   The New
York Herald thereafter called us "Mr. Beecher's
nigger minstrels," which served us well as an
advertisement.

Later on we met Mr. Beecher in New Haven,
where he and we were billed for the same evening,
he to lecture and we, of course, to sing.   We did not
know of his lecture in time, or we should never have
dared to go.   But luck was with us, for so few tickets
were sold for the lecture that it was called off, and

we were given a new proof of the greatness of this
man.   He attended our concert, made a speech and
was delighted to have these ex-slave children outdraw
him in that university town.

I thought him that night the grandest man in
the world.

A GROUP
OF APPRECIATIONS OF
MR. BEECHER

Mr. Beecher's grave, Greenwood Cemetery, Brooklyn

APPRECIATIONS OF MR. BEECHER

IT was my privilege to know Mr. Beecher well, and to be associated with him as only a few others were in some of the most critical periods of his life. He spoke in my church, and often graciously invited me to supply his pulpit, both in his presence and in his absence. Nearly if not quite the last lecture that he ever delivered was in the Montclair church. I shall never forget the walk to the train after that lecture. He said, " Let the carriage go, I would rather walk," and throwing his arm around my neck he walked and soliloquized. The shadow of his approaching departure already seemed to have touched him. He said, " Just think of it! I have been pastor of Plymouth Church nearly forty years, but I shall not be much longer." And then he talked about its future and his love for it, and seemed to be like one whose spirit was in some far-distant land. One day when we were talking about his difficulties and consequent labors, he said, " I will take care of the work if you will take care of the worry."

In a conference concerning the composition of his great council an objection was raised to the inviting of one well-known man because he was supposed to have prejudged the case; Mr. Beecher quickly said, " No! he is a fair man, and I will trust him, whatever his prejudgments." I heard him preach in the midst of his trial. There was not the faintest reference to what he was passing through. He seemed to be living in another world. His text was, " Seek ye first the kingdom of God," etc. Major Pond once told me of an afternoon ride with Mr. Beecher over the prairies. For an hour or two he was silent and absorbed, when, just

as the sun was setting, he turned toward the Major, put his
hand on his knees, and said, with tears in his eyes, " Pond,
just think of it; in a little while I shall see Jesus!" Major
Pond could not tell that story with an undimmed eye.

I was too near to Mr. Beecher in my early manhood
to be impartial now. He was more than any other like a
father in the ministry, often doing me thoughtful and un-
sought favors, and he was the same to a host of other young
ministers. He never forgot that he was young once, and
the less that any of us were able to do in return the more
ungrudging his service to us. As I think of him now the
qualities of his character which most impress me were his
generosity, his fairness, his love for his enemies, and, strange
as it may seem, his self-control. His own charity surpassed
any that he preached. As an orator he was unapproach-
able. I have heard most of the great pulpit orators of our
time and language — Punshon, Simpson, Spurgeon, Liddon,
Brooks, Parker — and not one could be compared with him.
I have seen great audiences bow before his eloquence as a
field of wheat goes down before the west wind.

As a preacher, in his combination of philosophic insight,
spiritual vision and power of persuasion, he was without a
peer. I do not think he was an original thinker; he had
no time for original work. But he absorbed that which was
best and most vital in the works of the original thinkers,
and in a true and noble sense became their interpreter, and
also an inspirer of thought as well as a molder of life. I
do not compare him with any other man whom our country
has produced, because he belongs in a class by himself.
The years are already driving away the clouds from his
memory. As an orator, a preacher, a patriot and a Christian, I believe that his name will endure as one of the most
precious possessions of the American people.

AMORY H. BRADFORD.

Montclair, New Jersey.

I KNEW Mr. Beecher as a preacher and as an orator, especially upon political and economic subjects. I was reared in the Episcopal Church and amongst old-time Democratic surroundings. Before I had heard or seen Mr. Beecher I was rather prejudiced against him. Curiosity first prompted me, as a very young man, to visit Plymouth Church. I entered with doubt and misgiving. I left, a disciple and a follower.

The crowds which went to hear him, notably during the period of excitement attendant upon the dark days of the great trial, often made it difficult to secure a seat or even to gain access to the building. I frequently sat upon the steps leading to the platform upon which he stood. Though inconvenient, my seat gave me the opportunity of hearing every word and of observing every change of expression in his wonderfully mobile countenance. Mr. Beecher was as much an actor as a preacher. Unconsciously every spoken sentence was reflected in action. His mouth was singularly expressive, and his full eye lighted with joy, flashed with indignation, or became suffused with tears, according to the varying moods of his marvelous oratory. I do not believe that there ever was another man possessing so large a share of originality as a speaker. Furthermore, if there ever was an impromptu orator Beecher was that man.

But the man himself was much more than his genius in moving audiences. Every one can trace much of his mental and moral make-up to original impulses derived from contact with great souls, in his family, his school, or college — amongst his teachers or even amongst strangers. Thus Mr. Beecher, years before I knew him, moved me in many ways.

He was one of the few men whom I have met whose reputation of greatness did not suffer by personal contact. He carried about him the atmosphere of a great man — something which cannot be defined, but only felt. He

taught me to throw off the bonds of traditional or conven-
tional thinking, and to think as a free man.   Then how new
and beautiful appeared to me the gospel of Jesus Christ!

He had the courage of his convictions in religion, eco-
nomics and in politics — and he made other men as brave
as himself.   In the prime of life, he fought the battle for
free men.   When the shadows were lengthening, with the
resilience of youth, he began a battle for free trade — to
restore to commerce the conditions designed by the Creator.
When asked as to whether he would like to live his long
life over again, he answered that he would not, but added,
in substance, " I should like to live long enough to induce
the American people to favor the unshackling of intercourse
between nation and nation."

It was my privilege to be the first secretary of the Reve-
nue Reform Club of Brooklyn, of which Mr. Beecher was
first president, and which, under his leadership, soon gained
a national reputation.   I came in frequent contact with him
then, and many a time heard him speak after such masters
of accurate and logical statement as David A. Wells and
Prof. William G. Sumner, using largely their material.   But
how different it all seemed when transmuted into humor and
satire, into fancy and imagery !

Mr. Beecher never could handle figures correctly, but
he nevertheless saw the philosophy and poetry which un-
derlay mathematics, and even the dryest statistics.   Men
like Mr. Wells instructed — but Beecher awakened the emotions which led to action.   I owe no man a larger debt of
gratitude, mainly, as I have intimated, because he taught
me to stand for what I believe to be right, and having
done all, still to stand.

It was my pleasure to suggest and to contribute to the
raising of the statue of Mr. Beecher which stands in the
busiest center of Brooklyn.   When Dr. Hillis, on New
Year's Day last, suggested a further memorial to his dis-

Beecher Statue, City Hall, Brooklyn, N. Y.

Beecher Memorial Church, Brooklyn, N. Y., toward the construction of which money was received from every state and territory in this country, from Canada, Scotland, England, Wales, Sweden, Denmark, South America, China and India.

tinguished predecessor — I felt it a pleasure to cooperate.
All who owe a debt to one of the greatest men of our time
should, by their generous contributions, see to it that the
Memorial worthily calls to mind the life-work of Henry
Ward Beecher.

FRED W. HINRICHS.

Brooklyn, New York.

I AM hardly to be counted among those who are entitled
to speak from a personal knowledge of Mr. Beecher. I
knew him with an affectionate admiration, but can only
claim that intimacy of acquaintance with him which is
due to the fact that all contact with him was intimate. So
much I ought to say if I venture to comment at all upon
his character. I would not undertake to pronounce an opinion upon the weight and scope of his intellectual powers; I
was always too eager a learner from him to think of measur-
ing his spiritual dimensions. I can only testify that my
contact with him — without the slightest knowledge of the
fact on his part, I feel sure — reshaped my life when I had
reached years where not many lives are reshaped. I think
those who knew him best will testify that he unconsciously
exercised this influence upon an amazing number of men.

Whatever his genius was, I shall presume no further
than to name three obvious characteristics which combined
to give that genius its fullest potency upon the vast numbers
of men whom he reached by his voice or with his pen :
First, his faultless and splendid courage, a three-fold courage of body, mind and heart, always perfectly balanced
with a spontaneous and absolutely unostentatious magnanimity ; next, the great dignity of his inmost spirit, joined
with a mirthful — a boyish — carelessness for outward sem-
blances ; and last, the yearning tenderness, the profundity
and the catholicity of his affections.

G. W. CABLE.

Northampton, Massachusetts.

I ALWAYS loved Mr. Beecher. Once when I was in great need of sympathy Mr. Beecher met me in Brooklyn on the street. He stopped, took my hand in both of his and expressed his warm regard for me, and encouraged me more than I can express by an inspiration not only from his words, but from the soul that appeared in his face and in all his framework.

I never went to hear him speak — and I went many times — that I did not come away with the expression, "What a manly man!" One of the first sermons that I heard from his lips after graduating from West Point, when I was on my way to an active campaign in Florida, was delivered in Plymouth Church, Brooklyn. Just before its close he brought his hand down upon the large Bible and said in substance, "I believe the teachings of that Book with all my heart." His attitude, his gesture and the tones of his voice impressed me in a way I could not forget. Of course I am but one of the multitude who were influenced by him to treasure up the words of eternal life.

In deed and in truth Henry Ward Beecher was a man like David, inspired by the Spirit of the Lord, and a man fearless in the proclamation of truth, but always in accordance with the great Master's own spirit.

OLIVER OTIS HOWARD.

Burlington, Vermont.

IT was my privilege to see Mr. Beecher many times, to have much pleasant talk with him, to hear him many times and on some great occasions; but I heard him preach only a few times. One of these puts out the light of all the others with its supreme magnificence. I think it must have been the best sermon that he ever preached. It was on the "Voice of God." It was as transcendental as Emerson. The doctrine was that the perpetual revelation is independent of all special revelations; that without Bible, Christ or Church the voice of God would have made itself heard in all lands and times. This doctrine was quite other than that of the deliberate agnosticism of his famous, "Can Theodore Parker Worship My God?" with the answer that he (Beecher) knew no God but Christ. It was the deliberate agnosticism of this doctrine that made Herbert Spencer's doctrine of the Unknowable so attractive to him. But a happy inconsistency saved him from the habitual expression of his deliberate theology. His heart was wiser than his head, and the language of that was the language of his sermon on the "Voice of God," not that of his theological contention that, except for Christ, we are without God in the world.

The poetry and humor of the man were for me his most remarkable traits. A good judge of these things once said to me, "Beecher has said more Shakespearean things than any one since Shakespeare." I think not, yet I should hardly know where to turn for one exceeding him. It is because these things do not inhere in a meditated body of thought that he is not now more widely read. He had the fatal gift of spontaneity — fatal to his literary permanence. He exerts his influence not through the medium of his writings, but through thousands of men and women who do not generally know whence they derive their help. He is "the sweet presence of a good diffused," by those who caught their inspiration from his living lips and from his writings when they were hot with the pulsation of his mighty heart.

His preaching was a dissolving agent, acting with immense force on the Calvinism which was dominant when he began to preach. I think he did not so much see "the glory of God in the face of Jesus Christ" as he saw the humanity of Jesus in the face of God. Perhaps this was not sound theology, but it presented a human ideal of entrancing beauty, and the ideals men honor are dynamic

forces in their lives. Henry Ward Beecher's Jesus was a
great improvement upon Calvin's . God, much more con-
straining to all noble things.

JOHN WHITE CHADWICK.

Brooklyn, New York.

I REMEMBER in Mr. Beecher's preaching a wonderful
vitality which made the truths of religion in his handling
to be felt as matters of near and immediate interest.
Elizabeth Barrett Browning, writing of her husband's
earlier volume, " Bells and Pomegranates," says :

> Or of Browning, some pomegranate which, if cut deep down
>   the middle,
> Shows a heart within blood-tinctured of a veined humanity.

These lines express for me the impression of Mr.
Beecher's personality which I derived from his sermons.
I had heard him from time to time before the Civil War,
always with great pleasure and interest, but I must think
that the inspiration of that great contest brought out in
him a new power and fervor. Preachers often impress us
with their remoteness from our common human life. In
their sermons we seem to smell the very leather of the
volumes which are their daily and hourly companions.
Mr. Beecher spoke to us from the heart of the life of his
own time, interpreting to us its duties and its lessons.

Never shall I forget one occasion early in the Civil War
when I found a seat in one of the crowded pews of a congregation waiting and eager to hear him. His discourse
was so uplifting and inspiring in its character that it seemed
to find a fit culmination in the hymn that followed its close :

> We are living, we are dwelling,
>   In a strange and awful time,
> In an age on ages telling, —
>   To be living is sublime.

I recall another Sunday in the days in which an out-

rageous scandal which assailed Mr. Beecher was at its
height. I happened to be visiting at the house of a friend
who did not feel the assurance which I felt of the infamous
falsehood of the charges preferred against the great teacher.
In spite of her earnest persuasion I took my way to Plymouth Church to attend its morning service. I must confess
that I did this with some trouble of mind, saying to myself,
"If there is any truth in these charges, I shall feel it in the
insincerity which will naturally show itself in the utterances
of the preacher." As I entered the church a heavenly calm
seemed to rest upon the congregation. The splendid choir
began Mendelssohn's beautiful chorus:

> He, watching over Israel,
> Slumbers not, nor sleeps.

I waited with some anxiety for the first words of the pastor's
prayer. In them I found the same calm, the same uplifting
trust in the divine Guardian. My thought was, "This man
stands in the innermost refuge of the Just; the citadel of
a conscience void of offense against God or man."

I remember a word of Mr. Beecher's which I chanced
to hear in what were to me rather heedless days. It was
to the following effect: "Do not suppose that at a time
when you may keenly feel the need of religious comfort
and help you will be able to command them as one orders
a suit of clothes from a tailor." This homely simile so
impressed me that I have carried it with me ever since.
Not very long after my hearing it a severe family affliction
brought it vividly to my mind, from which the lesson intended has never vanished.

From time to time Mr. Beecher used to come to Boston
in order to fulfill some lecture engagement. On one of
these occasions a lady friend, meeting me in the street,
said: "Mr. Beecher has come to town to-day, and I cannot
well entertain him. Do you think of any one who would
like to invite him to dinner?"—the hour of which in those

days was two o'clock. I replied that I should be most happy to receive him at my house. Hastening to invite a friend to meet him, I prefaced my invitation with these words, " The sun is going to rise in my parlor to-day — Henry Ward Beecher is coming to dine with me." This friend was Mary Booth, the charming wife of the great tragedian, Edwin Booth. When, not long afterwards, Mrs. Booth was stricken with sudden and fatal disease, Mr. Beecher wrote to her husband a very kind and consoling letter.

What I have here written only seems to me to show that words can but partially express the charm and power of those unique personalities which illuminate the world of their time, and, passing, leave behind them a track of light which bears witness to what they did, but cannot recall what they were.

JULIA WARD HOWE.

Boston, Massachusetts.

THE charm of Channing was profound and indescribable. But Henry Ward Beecher recalls Whitefield more than any other renowned preacher. Like Whitefield, he was what is known as a man of the people; a man of strong virility, of exuberant vitality, of quick sympathy, of an abounding humor, of a rapid play of poetic imagination, of great fluency of speech; an emotional nature overflowing in ardent expression, of strong convictions, of complete self-confidence; but also not sensitive, nor critical, nor judicial; a hearty, joyous nature, touching ordinary human life at every point, and responsive to every generous moral impulse.

GEORGE WILLIAM CURTIS.

MR. BEECHER was as genuine an American as ever walked through a field of Indian corn. He had not the fine fiber of the scholastic thoroughbred, but he had the hearty manhood of Lincoln.

OLIVER WENDELL HOLMES.